Blueprints
FOR THE
Little Church

Creating an Orthodox Home

ELISSA BJELETICH & CALEB SHOEMAKER

ANCIENT FAITH PUBLISHING ✝ CHESTERTON, INDIANA

Blueprints for the Little Church: Creating an Orthodox Home
Copyright © 2016 by Elissa Bjeletich and Caleb Shoemaker

Published by:
  Ancient Faith Publishing
  A Division of Ancient Faith Ministries
  P.O. Box 748
  Chesterton, IN 46304

ISBN: 978-1-944967-00-0

Printed in the United States of America

Contents

Ask Your Priest

As you make your way through this book, you may have questions. Please, ask your priest.

As you attempt to implement the concepts you find here, you may run into trouble. Whenever you're in doubt, please ask your priest.

No book can take the place of the active, pastoral care of a priest. No book knows you, prays for you, or sees you. Your priest does.

The Church loves you. You've been assigned your own shepherd, a spiritual father tasked with guiding you, keeping you on the narrow path. What a wonderful gift! Go talk with him. Ask your priest.

Don't say, "Bible-reading is for monks; am I turning my child into a monk?" No! It isn't necessary for him to be a monk. Make him into a Christian! Why are you afraid of something so good? It is necessary for everyone to know Scriptural teachings, and this is especially true for children. Even at their age they are exposed to all sorts of folly and bad examples from popular entertainments. Our children need remedies for all these things! We are so concerned with our children's schooling; if only we were equally zealous in bringing them up in the discipline and instruction of the Lord! And then we wonder why we reap such bitter fruit when we have raised our children to be insolent, licentious, impious and vulgar. May this never happen; instead, let us heed the blessed Paul's admonition to bring them up in the discipline and instruction of the Lord. Let us give them a pattern to imitate; from their earliest years let us teach them to study the Bible.

—St. John Chrysostom[1]

Introduction

This book offers hope to those engaged in the struggle against the passions. It is imperfect advice penned for imperfect people, warring to make sense of a dark and mysterious world through the lens of the Orthodox faith. Among the myriad voices trying to tell you what to think and how to act, among the countless sources of monastic wisdom and patristic treasures, among the countless Pinterest boards and parenting blogs, this book makes a humble offering to mothers and fathers who wish to see their family embrace the Orthodox faith and to raise living saints.

This is a book for parents. It is for newly minted parents and for seasoned veterans of the struggle to raise godly children; for recently illumined Orthodox converts, and for cradle Orthodox who have rediscovered the depth and wealth of the Orthodox Church for themselves and wish to bring their families to a place of holiness and piety. We offer this book from sincere hearts to you who desire to present the rich heritage of the Orthodox Church's teachings for families—what our great saints and elders have often called "the little church."

Throughout this book we will engage the conversation of how to build our little church with personal stories, advice, and encouragements from Orthodox parents who are walking along with you in the struggle for holiness. This book is structured on the three foundation stones of the Christian life as described in Scripture and our Tradition. These three foundation stones for your little church are prayer, fasting, and almsgiving. Though we will address other important elements in your family's spiritual development, these three essential disciplines will form the foundation for every piece of your family's growth. Look at this quote from the Old Testament, where the Archangel Raphael offers advice for living a righteous life:

> Do good, and evil will not find you. Prayer is good with fasting, almsgiving, and righteousness. A few prayers with righteousness are better than many with wrongdoing. It is better to do almsgiving than to lay up gold. For almsgiving rescues one from death, and it will wash away every sin. Those who do almsgiving and are righteous will be full of life. But those who sin are enemies of their own life. (Tobit 12:7–10)

Indeed, in the Sermon on the Mount, Jesus gives prayer, fasting, and almsgiving preeminence among the disciplines of the Kingdom of God (see Matt. 6).

Where Do We Begin?

For the convert to Orthodoxy or for those raised Orthodox who wish to revitalize their faith, getting started can be overwhelming. With diverse local and ethnic traditions and so many pious practices available to the Orthodox family, it's hard to know where to start. Orthodox parents need a road map to navigate this maze. Which of these things are really necessary to a good Orthodox life, and which are not?

For many families, it is hard enough to get the family up and out of bed for the Divine Liturgy each week—let alone to take on daily prayer, frequent Scripture reading, weekly fasting, Lenten seasons, Vespers, vigils, Matins, and feast days! How can we do everything we're "supposed to do" when it's hard enough to find time to do the bare minimum? How are we to raise saints when our toddler doesn't want to keep his diaper on?

There's never a point at which it's too late. With anything—careers, hairstyles, musical taste, changing diet or exercise habits—there's nothing to prevent us from taking a look over the horizon and pushing the reset button on our lives. At any time of the year, any day of the week, we can decide the direction we are heading needs to shift and take definite actions to redirect our course. Blessed Fr. Seraphim Rose so plainly put it, "God's revelation is given to something called a loving heart." Begin here—pray, and allow God's revelation to be given to you and warm you to the process of turning your family toward God.

For many young families and new converts, the pressure to do it right overrides good sense. Rather than make small adjustments and begin to move slowly toward a regular prayer rule, fasting, attendance at services, and so forth, we try to do everything at once, only to wind up with spiritual indigestion. Hopefully, as you read this book, you'll find you can make the shift slowly, in such a way that your family doesn't pay the price and you don't burn yourself out.

The key ingredient in building your little church is to avoid comparing yourself to anyone else. Everyone's piety is personal; it's between them and God—and hopefully their confessor. It's not one-size-fits-all, and just as you can't expect to try on someone else's custom-made leather gloves and expect them to fit—well, like a glove—you shouldn't expect someone else's prayer rule to fit you perfectly, either. There are countless resources online and in print for developing a pious Orthodox life, but nothing can compare to a personal conversation with your priest or father confessor, who can guide you through the process.

As I came into the Church and learned about the faith, I began to feel discouraged. Every time our family had made some progress, I'd hear some story or comment from another parishioner and realize that our small steps were tiny compared to the wonderful spiritual life they were leading. I felt like they knew saints and writers of whom I'd never heard, and I worried that their children were better behaved and more pious than my own. My wise priest advised me to stop comparing, to know that we are all running this race together but we must run it with our heads down. When I stopped worrying about what others were doing, I was better able to focus and to lead my own family. In time I came to understand that every family has its own unique struggles, and that even my most impressive friends were facing challenges I could not see. —Elissa

In every part of this book, we offer the same advice: Ask your priest. There's a real danger in getting carried away trying to accomplish great things on your own without guidance. Don't. Don't do this alone. Don't damage your family's spiritual life. Don't leave room for pride. Before you do it, ask your priest.

One of the hardest things I've ever had to do as a parent was to ask for help. We were struggling with a lot of things in our personal and spiritual lives when we were a young family, and it was often the children who suffered most from Mom and Dad's struggles to balance money, jobs, church, family, and other responsibilities. I remember feeling very helpless and wishing someone would come along and just rescue us from all the hardships. No one ever did. No Superman came to save the day and make our problems go away. What did happen was much more humbling, but much more empowering to us as parents: People stepped in and showed us where we were losing touch. People helped us to see that (much to our chagrin) we were failing to love our children well and were not showing them the love of Christ. It took these "busybody" people in our lives to show us we'd lost step with what was most important to us. We finally swallowed all that parental pride and made efforts to get counseling and help from our priest, who showed us how to walk a balanced life with our families. Don't be afraid to ask for help. You'll never know what your family can accomplish when you seek counsel and guidance along the path. —Caleb

The Family—The Little Church

The preparation of the Temple, the preparation of the dispassionate flame, must begin within ourselves, with a recognition of who we are. "And how is your little church doing? How are matushka and the children?" Such a greeting, common among Orthodox Christians, may seem confusing to those outside the Church. The *ecclesia*, the body of believers, makes up the Holy Church. The family is the "little church," an icon of the life of the entire ecclesia in Christ. A building prepared for use as the Temple is consecrated by the bishop. Likewise, when we have prepared a residence for our family, we ask the priest to bless it, for it is to be the dwelling place of our little church.

When we enter a Temple, we see before us the icon screen. When we enter an Orthodox Christian home, we see the *krasny ugol*, the "beautiful corner," as the Russians call it, or icon corner. While it may not be directly opposite the entrance, it is not hidden away, for it is the center of our family life: Here we give thanks to God for having brought us through the night, we ask for God to guide us through the day, we ask for God's blessings as we begin activities throughout the day—be they taking a meal, undertaking a task or setting out on a journey—and we give thanks to God upon their completion. Here we keep holy water and prosphora (blessed bread) to be taken at the beginning of each day. Here we see the images of the saints whose names we bear and who are praying with us and for us. Here, in maintaining the lamps before the icons, we reinforce each day the lesson which that priest so simply and eloquently expressed. "O gentle light . . ."[2]

Jesus said to him, "You shall love the LORD your God with all your heart, with all your soul, and with all your mind." (Matt. 22:37)

What Is an Orthodox Life?

In our modern culture, we compartmentalize our lives: we consider our work lives and personal lives, family time and "me" time as distinct from one another. Some of us set aside Sunday mornings for our religious time. Some of us may even take the time on Saturday nights for Vespers or try to observe Great Lent. We believe that if each of these separate aspects of our lives can be healthy and fulfilling, we will have lived a good life.

Yet Jesus clearly calls us to love Him with all our heart, all our soul, and all our mind. There is no compartmentalization in this, but true unity. Every aspect of ourselves and our lives should be united in our love for the Lord. Instead of seeing ourselves as a fragmented collection of various identities, Christ is calling us to a unified understanding of ourselves and our lives. Love for God must become the foundation of everything, and all aspects of our lives—our jobs and our families and our recreation, our meals and our entertainment—must all be connected to and part of a unified whole. We must build up our lives and our hearts and raise our families on the foundation of our faith.

Orthodoxy offers a means of bringing each element of our lives into our relationship with God. We baptize our children and bless our homes; we sanctify our diets with fasting and feed our minds with Scripture and the teachings of the Fathers. In the Church, we find the means to incorporate every aspect of ourselves into one good life. The word *wholesome* literally indicates a healthy wholeness, a unity that is good for us. Children benefit from the wholesomeness of a family life dedicated to the love of God.

> What saves and makes for good children is the life of the parents in the home. The parents need to devote themselves to the love of God. They need to become saints in their relations to their children through their mildness, patience, and love. They need to make a new start every day, with a fresh outlook, renewed enthusiasm and love for their children. And the joy that will come to them, the holiness that will visit them, will shower grace on their children. —St. Porphyrios[3]

Parents must become saints, and grace will be showered on their children! That's not an easy road, and it's difficult to achieve in the climate of our modern culture.

None of this is to suggest that the domestic church is a necessarily peaceful and magical place; becoming the domestic church is no supernatural formula, and its prayers are not magical incantations that will produce harmony and joy. Family life is a struggle, no matter what; but when we struggle with Christ, we reap rewards. The work of shepherding a family is relentless and tiresome, but when we understand ourselves as the little church, we begin to see blessings even in the struggles. This is no magic potion to make life easy, but simply another of the ways in which patience and work reap benefits later.

The American way of thinking and making decisions is growing ever more secular, moving away from a traditional religious perspective. Recently, the Pew Research Center released information regarding the status of Christianity and religion in the United States, and among those traditions studied, Orthodox Christians have one of the lowest rates of retention across Christian and non-Christian denominations. Only 53% of adults who were raised in the Orthodox Church still identify themselves as Orthodox Christians, which means that roughly half of all children raised in Orthodox households have left the Church.[4] Many factors play into this statistic, but it should be eye-opening to Orthodox Christian parents who are working to build their little church. We need to think about how we are raising our children and whether we are truly planting the faith in their hearts.

These statistics could be discouraging to both family and parish, or they can be seen as a wake-up call, an incredible opportunity for growth and real commitment to the faith. In light of these revealing statistics, Barna Group—along with other independent and denominational think tanks—have pinpointed key factors in those children who retain the faith in which they were raised:

» Mentoring relationships with non-parent adults
» Teaching cultural discernment
» Involvement of young people within the church
» Vocational discipleship
» A personal encounter with Jesus

Of the five things listed by Barna, four are completely within the grasp of parents. How empowering! Parents provide many of the elements that nurture authentic, lasting membership in the Church. Indeed, the reality is that young people are fleeing the faith of their families, but not those whose families have instilled a deep faith within their hearts; and the little church is one of the defining reasons children stay in the Church as they grow up.

Review that list from Barna again: What are the elements that enable children to develop a vibrant faith? How many of them are native to Orthodox Christian spirituality? Godparents are meant to provide a meaningful relationship with non-parent adults. Boys and girls cans serve in various ways in the parish, from altar servers to planning events and working to maintain the beauty of the parish. The Church addresses every cultural question a person may have—not just ethnic culture, but questions of morality and holiness. Vocational discipleship can be fostered through a relationship with a caring father confessor, Sunday school teacher, or monastic father or mother. Our Divine Liturgy is designed around a personal and corporate encounter with God as we serve before Him and partake of the Sacraments.

The only one of the five items identified by Barna over which a parent has no control is the last. We cannot provide a meaningful experience with God for our children. We can prepare the ground, present them with opportunities, share our own experiences, but we cannot encounter Christ for them—they must do that for themselves. We can lead them to water, and we can tell them what it means to thirst and talk about how satisfying the water has been in our own lives, but they must decide to drink.

> Holy Scripture says of the midwives who kept alive the Israelites' male children, that through the God-fearing midwives they made themselves houses. Does it mean they made visible houses? How can they say they acquired houses through the fear of God when we do the opposite, and learn in time, through fear of God to give up the houses we have? Evidently this does not refer to visible houses but to the houses of the soul which each one builds for himself by keeping God's commandments.

Through this Holy Scripture teaches us that the fear of God prepares the soul to keep the commandments, and through the commandments the house of the soul is built up. Let us take hold of them, brothers, and let us fear God, and we shall build houses for ourselves where we shall find shelter in winter weather, in the season of storm-cloud, lightning, and rain; for not to have a home in winter-time is a great hardship. —St. Dorotheos of Gaza

The Orthodox life is not complicated. It is beautiful in its simplicity, wondrous in its depth, vivifying in its ritual and sacraments. The complications are typically self-imposed when, instead of following the Church's teachings or the admonitions of our priests and confessors, we try to cobble together a hodge-podge religion based mostly on external trappings and false deadlines.

It is in this milieu that the Pew research becomes the most startling and the Barna findings become most empowering. You don't have to do this alone! You aren't responsible for finding the correct path in the dark. As you build your little church and your family grows in grace, you will find that the path is clearly marked, and you are free to walk it at your own pace. Trust is key to this lifestyle. Trust your priest; trust the Church's Tradition; trust yourself, remembering these words of sacred Scripture:

I thank God, whom I serve with a pure conscience, as *my* forefathers *did*, as without ceasing I remember you in my prayers night and day, greatly desiring to see you, being mindful of your tears, that I may be filled with joy, when I call to remembrance the genuine faith that is in you, which dwelt first in your grandmother Lois and your mother Eunice, and I am persuaded is in you also. (2 Tim. 1:3–5)

CHAPTER 1

Why the Little Church?

For indeed a house is a little Church. Thus it is possible for us by becoming good husbands and wives to surpass all others.

—St. John Chrysostom[5]

The Church does not refer to a building or a single parish community, nor to an enormous multinational organization with a structure of patriarchs and metropolitans and priests. As we Orthodox know it, the Church is a mystery: it is the Body of Christ, a holy communion of the saints in heaven and all of us still struggling in this life, reaching across time and space.

The larger Church is led by Christ, whose authority passes down through patriarchs and bishops, all organized into patriarchates and dioceses and parishes. But the parish is not the smallest unit; it is further divided into families known as "little churches."

In the marriage ceremony, the new husband and wife are crowned, both as martyrs for the sacrifices they will make and as the rightful leaders of their new household, their little church. Christ is invited inside to become the center and the head of the little church, just as He is both center and head of the larger Church. The little church has its own hierarchy and its lay versions of the sacraments—we break bread together, we bless one another, anoint one another, pray for one another, and love one another in this little community, striving together to grow ever closer to Christ.

As with all the services in our parish church, we dedicate every activity of the little church to God. We pray for His blessing before everything we do. (As we say in the Divine Liturgy, "Let us commend ourselves and one another and our whole lives unto Christ our God." Not "let us commend our Sunday mornings," but "let us commend our whole lives unto Christ our God.") That moment when we make the conscious decision to cross ourselves in the name of the Father, Son, and Holy Spirit, we move from being individuals to becoming the tangible Body of Christ in whatever situation we happen to find ourselves.

The Little Church in the Modern World

> The fact that I am a monk and you are a layman is of no importance. The Lord listens equally to the monk and to the man of the world provided both are true believers. He looks for a heart full of true faith into which to send his Spirit. For the heart of a man is capable of containing the Kingdom of God. The Holy Spirit and the Kingdom of God are one. —St. Seraphim of Sarov

The life of a monastic is entirely devoted to God; the monastery's rhythm calls one to prayer at regular intervals, structuring the day with room for holy services. It's easy to imagine that such a life leads one to great holiness—and it can. St. Anthony fled the beautiful cities of Egypt to live among the dead in the desert tombs in order to obey the commandment of Christ and attain perfection. St. Silouan the Athonite took the promises of the Theotokos to Mt. Athos and fled his earthly life to embrace the angelic life of the monastery.

Family life, however, can also lead one to deep spirituality. A family can be immersed in prayer, both at table and after, and their hospitality and generosity will speak of an earnest application of Christ's exhortation to love their neighbor as themselves.

Of course, this isn't common in the twenty-first century. Our modern family homes offer very little stillness; we move frenetically from one activity to the next, and our loud lives seem to have nothing in common with the monastic life. Family households are dominated by relentless, redundant tasks—we cook a meal and serve it, only to clean it up and then make another one in a few hours; we tidy a room only to have it immediately torn apart by active children; we carefully put away bicycles, basketballs, and jump ropes only to find them scattered in the driveway an hour later. The work of the family never seems to stay done: everything we accomplish will be undone and accomplished again shortly. It doesn't fit the quiet garden of the monastery cloister as we imagine it.

> Or, a mother asks God to grant her patience. Her little child then comes in, and as soon as she has the table set for dinner, he pulls on the table cloth and everything spills on the floor. At such times it's as if the child is saying to his mother: "Mama, be patient!" —St. Paisios[6]

In some ways it feels as if we cannot accomplish anything spiritual, because we are always called back to these redundant tasks.

The truth is quite the opposite, however. Think about the traditional monastery: This community, this space, is set aside for worship and contemplation of God. The monastics engage in simple, repetitive work, with regular interruptions from the talanton or the bells, which call them away from their work to prayer. Parents engage in redundant tasks and find themselves called away from their own thoughts and plans by their children. Both environments are designed to call us away from our own egos and our own plans, drawing us to prayer. Perhaps the family home is not so different from the monastery.

> In everything and at every time strive to please God. [. . .] On rising from your bed, make the sign of the Cross and say: "In the name of the Father, the Son and the Holy Spirit," and also, "Vouchsafe, O Lord, to keep us this day without sin and teach me to do Thy will." While washing, either at home or at the baths, say: "Purge me with hyssop, Lord, and I shall be clean; wash me and I shall be whiter than snow." When putting on your linen, think of the cleanliness of the heart, and ask the Lord for a clean heart: "Create in me a clean heart, O God!" If you have made new clothes and are putting them on, think of the renewal of the spirit and say: "Renew a right spirit within me"; laying aside old clothes, and disdaining them, think with still greater disdain of laying aside the old man, the sinful, passionate, carnal man. Tasting the sweetness of bread, think of the true bread, which gives eternal life to the soul—the Body and Blood of Christ—and hunger after this bread—that is, long to communicate of it oftener. Drinking water, tea, sweet-tasting mead or any other drink, think of the true drink that quenches the thirst of the soul. [. . .] When you are going anywhere, think of the righteousness of spiritually walking before God and say: "Order my steps in Thy word and let not any iniquity have dominion

over me." When doing anything, strive to do it with the thought
of God, the Creator, who has made everything by His infinite
wisdom, grace and omnipotence, and has created you after His
image and likeness. —St. John of Kronstadt[7]

God sends everything to us for our salvation, and we can receive
it that way, accepting each of our daily tasks and experiences as
a call to prayer. When confronted with mountains of laundry,
we can thank God for clothing us as He clothes the lilies of the
field; when approaching a sink full of dirty dishes, we can thank
Him for providing food and ask that He nourish our souls as
well. Every mundane task that makes family life so busy can be
received as a call to prayer.

> On the Holy Mountain, as we said earlier, whether one is
> working or doing his handicraft or praying in church, everything
> becomes a prayer. And we who are here in the world, who have
> a family, a wife and children, we have to do our jobs, and our
> very jobs, our work, become a prayer—just like a monk when
> he does his prayer rule: he gets up, he falls down, he gets up, he
> falls down; he doesn't seem to be doing anything, and yet that is
> prayer. —Archimandrite Vasileios of Iveron[8]

Every task becomes a prayer—even washing the dishes and scrub-
bing the floors—when we are prayerful while we are working.

If we can accomplish this, our homes will truly be transformed
into little churches, communities set aside for God. Our work
will become sanctifying like the simple work of the monastics,
and the cries of our children will call us away from our self-
centered thoughts and our own will to service and love. All the
parents' labor and sacrifice, which once seemed to be a barrier to

holiness, is put to its intended good use and becomes our offering to God. The family home becomes a most organic and natural monastery, a truly sacred space in which our lives are dedicated to spiritual growth and nurturing.

> We got ready and went over to the church. On going in we at once saw the lady of the house, who had been there some time already with her children. We were all present at matins, and the Divine Liturgy went straight on afterward. The head of the house with his little boy and I took our places within the altar, while his wife and the little girl stood near the altar window, where they could see the elevation of the holy gifts. How earnestly they prayed as they knelt and shed tears of joy! And I wept to the full myself as I looked at the light on their faces. (*The Way of the Pilgrim*)[9]

We have an icon corner in the front room of our house. Icons of Christ and the Theotokos are to the right and left of our wall cross. Beneath is a two-level table. On top of the table are other icons of our patron saints and other saints to whom we feel close (is that a strange way to say it? You probably know what I mean). On the bottom level are bottles of holy water, palm crosses, and candles. —Becky, mother of two

The family unit is sacred. The husband and wife at their wedding are crowned as king and queen and are presented with the challenge to live sacrificially for one another, to raise up children, and to serve as a living icon of Christ and His Church. The children gather round their table like olive branches—or at least that's what the Psalmist says. It's this life-creating spiritual reality that so impresses the pilgrim in *The Way of the Pilgrim* and is such a challenge for Orthodox parents. The truth is that your home is a school, a hospital, and a church. Your children will learn their spirituality from you, and it is a sacred calling for parents to shepherd—literally, to pastor—their children in the ways of righteousness.

Wedding and Baptism

In the excitement and surreality of the moment, few of us remember—or pay very close attention to—the words of the prayers said over us and over our children at baptisms and weddings. It's not easy to remember all the admonitions and exhortations—the warnings, the encouragements—offered by the Church to godparents and parents, sponsors, and bride and groom when you're the one being admonished and exhorted.

Consequently, many of us begin life as parents or as a couple with an incomplete idea of what we are being sanctified to do. We are being set apart and sealed for one another and for the Kingdom of God for the purpose of raising up saints who will in turn raise up saints to the glory of God. That's a tall order!

In order to help you better understand the Church's teachings about marriage and family life, we've included some selections from the services of Matrimony, Baptism, and Chrismation. It's important to our conversation about becoming the little church that we realize what foundations were laid for us at the start of our families and early on in the lives of each of our children. Take time to consider these words and meditate on their meanings for you and your little church.

WEDDING PRAYERS

For the servants of God, who are now being joined to one another in the community of marriage, and for their salvation . . .

That there may be given unto them soberness of life, and fruit of the womb as may be most expedient for them . . .

That they may rejoice in beholding sons and daughters . . .

That there may be granted unto them the happiness of abundant fertility, and a course of life blameless and unashamed . . .

That there may be granted unto them and unto us all prayers that tend unto salvation . . .

That both they and we may be delivered from tribulation, wrath, danger, and necessity . . .

Bless this marriage and grant unto these Your servants a peaceful life, length of days, chastity, love for one another in a bond of peace, offspring long-lived, fair fame by reason of their children, and a crown of glory that does not fade away.

Account them worthy to see their children's children. Keep their wedlock safe against every hostile scheme; give them of the dew from the heavens above, and of the fatness of the earth. Fill their houses with bountiful food, and with every good thing, that they may have to give to them that are in need, bestowing also on them that are here assembled with us all their supplications that are unto salvation.

BAPTISM PRAYERS

Drive out from him (her) every evil and unclean spirit, hiding and lurking in his (her) heart. (3x) The spirit of error, the spirit of evil, the spirit of idolatry and of all covetousness that works according to the teaching of the devil. Make him (her) a reason-endowed sheep of the holy Flock of Your Christ, an honorable member of Your Church, a hallowed vessel, a child of Light, and heir of Your Kingdom. So that, having ordered his (her) life according to Your commandments, and having guarded the seal and kept it unbroken, and having preserved his (her) garment undefiled, he (she) may attain unto the blessedness of the saints of Your Kingdom. Through the grace and compassion and man-befriending love of Your Only-Begotten Son, with whom You are blessed, together with Your All-Holy, Good, and Life-creating Spirit, both now and ever, and to the ages of ages. Amen.

That he (she) may preserve the garment of Baptism, and the earnest of the Spirit undefiled and blameless in the terrible Day of Christ our God . . .

Form the Image of Your Christ in him (her) who is about to be born again through my humility. Build him (her) on the foundation of Your Apostles and Prophets. Cast him (her) not down, but plant him (her) as a plant of truth in Your Holy, Catholic, and Apostolic Church. Pluck him (her) not out, that by his (her) advancing in piety, by the same may be glorified Your Most Holy Name, of Father, and of Son, and of Holy Spirit, both now and ever, and to the ages of ages. Amen.

A robe of divine light bestow upon me, O You that for vesture array Yourself with Light; and bestow many mercies, O Christ our God, who are plenteous in mercy.

With each wedding and baptism we attend, we're reminded of the riches and blessings of family life. It is so beautiful: the participants dressed in white, the candles, the hymns, the flowers, the water, the oil. It's all so visceral and sensual that it's hard to grasp the real-world purpose of these elaborate rituals. It is in these moments—these holy spaces—that man and woman are no longer individuals but are bound to one another, and a new icon is created. It is in this holy event that a young child is crucified with Christ, resurrected with Him in glory, sealed with the Holy Spirit, and tonsured—set apart—for the work of the priesthood in which all believers participate.

Raising Saints

> Marriage is more than human. It is a [. . .] miniature kingdom which is the little house of the Lord.
>
> —St. Clement of Alexandria

How does all this translate to our everyday lives? When we become more aware of the work we are called to do; when we understand that we are meant to lead our household to Christ; when we begin to think differently about how we approach the various questions and situations we face, it is then that we begin to build on solid rock instead of on the seashore.

Becoming the little church means acquiring a new mindset. We are not simply raising children to live happy and healthy lives—we are raising saints who will find their rewards in heaven. This is radically different from the popular notion that we want "good kids" or "well-behaved kids." Moralism will only produce pharisees and passionless drones. The saints of God are filled with the Holy Spirit, radiate the Divine Light, and bring others to salvation.

The protagonist of L. M. Montgomery's Anne of Green Gables series is the precocious Anne Shirley—an eleven-year-old orphan taken in by an elderly brother and sister on Prince Edward Island in Canada. Her stories are well known to many of us through books and film, and an interesting analogy can be made between Anne's foibles and what we mean by raising holy children versus "good kids" who never cause mischief.

Anne's main provider and parent figure is the never-married, childless Marilla Cuthbert. An outwardly virtuous but inwardly dry woman, Marilla is initially exasperated by the scrapes Anne gets into, her wild swings of emotion, and the unconventional way she behaves. However, Marilla eventually comes to love Anne for her sincere virtue, her loving heart, her selflessness, and her love for her neighbor. Marilla herself is profoundly changed by knowing Anne—in fact, she learns how to love. Anne's exuberant love and joy eventually bring everyone around her to a fuller experience of life.

This is an excellent analogy to the raising of saints. Anne, imperfect and prone to mistakes, learns over time to control her temper, her tongue, her imagination, and her wild passions, and she brings blessings to both her guardians and the people around her, regardless of their position in society or her own. All children have their ups and downs. Some children are more even-tempered; others are more exuberant. Anne certainly has her faults, but her virtue shines through as she learns and matures.

How often do we parents, motivated by love for our children and by the pressures of society, compare our children to our neighbor's well-mannered children (whom we only ever see on their best behavior)?

When we are faced with decisions, whether they are about work or hobbies or child-rearing, our recognition that we are heads of this little church gives us a framework for reaching coherent and good answers. Like our parishes, our little churches should be communities always centered on Christ, where love and forgiveness reign, where we pray together and struggle toward salvation together. This includes directing our children in loving submission and repentance to their Heavenly Father, who has promised to complete a good work in them. It is not about manners—it's about holiness. It's not about "good behavior"—it's about a life given completely to God in loving humility and peace.

Ascesis of the Family

> Be magnified, O Bridegroom, as Abraham, and blessed as Isaac, and increased as was Jacob. Go your way in peace, performing in righteousness the commandments of God. And you, O Bride, be magnified as was Sarah, and rejoice as did Rebecca, and increase as did Rachel, being glad in your husband, keeping the paths of the Law, for so God is well pleased. (Orthodox Wedding Service)

Each one of us is called to be an ascetic—a spiritual athlete. Some of us are called to the monastic life, others to the married, and a select few are called to live as celibates in the world—those who have never married but live the so-called "secular" life of the professional or tradesperson. There is no middle ground between these. There is no Christian life that is not presented to us as training for eternity.

When we talk about ascesis, we tend to think of godly men and women who went out into the wilderness to live on whatever they could find and water the desert with weeping. That is not the only kind of ascesis, though. A look through Christian history and biblical examples will reveal another kind of holy life devoted to the ascetic practices of family. Some of these examples are obvious—maybe so obvious that they aren't immediately recognizable as ascesis when compared to, say, climbing a tower and refusing solid foods for thirty years.

Healthy Patterns and Holy Habits

Regular Church Attendance: Perhaps nothing is so basic to family spirituality as regular church attendance, and yet asking a family to add one more thing to their already busy schedule may seem daunting. Nothing can replace the regular liturgical worship of God's people; and nothing can be done outside the home which will do more for the development of godly children and for building your little church.

Prayer: Orthodox Christians are called to pray without ceasing. This means keeping God constantly before our minds and seeing Him and praising Him in all circumstances. This is not an easy task, but it is essential to training saints for their eternal lives.

Fasting: Regular fasting during Great Lent and other fasting periods may seem daunting at first, but by beginning with the two weekly fast days (Wednesday and Friday), you can build up your fasting gradually and prepare your family for the joy and spiritual benefits of abstinence and repentance.

Charitable Giving: Even outside the Church, it is understood that regular giving to charity is a sign of a healthy understanding of money and its use as a tool. People who give regularly are, overall, happier, healthier, and less prone to depression and fear when it comes to money.

It is the responsibility of each family to discover how they can add these ascetic practices to their daily routine. Sunday school, religious schools, and summer camps are not enough; they may enrich what you are doing in the home, but they cannot replace it. We cannot outsource the raising of saints. Families should incorporate holy habits as part of their daily, weekly, monthly, and yearly routines; this rhythm is what truly nourishes our children in the faith. It is a daunting task, but these are the building blocks of Scripture's wise man who built his house upon stone so that when the storms came down and the floods came up, the house on the rock stood firm. Children are a gift of the Lord, and blessed is the man whose quiver is full (see Ps. 126[127]:5); but having children is not the end of the equation—we are tasked with bringing them to Christ and encouraging the cultivation of holiness and piety in them through cooperation with the Holy Spirit.

> For the servant of God and the handmaiden of God who now pledge themselves to one another, and for their salvation; let us pray to the Lord. (Orthodox Wedding Service)

> If the man who buried his one talent gained nothing, but was punished instead, it is obvious that one's own virtue is not enough for salvation, but the virtue of those for whom we are responsible is also required. Therefore, let us be greatly concerned for our wives and our children, and for ourselves as well, and as we educate both ourselves and them let us beg God to help us in our task. If He sees that we care about this, He will help us. —St. John Chrysostom[10]

CHAPTER 2

Getting Started

*Don't worry too much about how spiritually poor you
are—God sees that, but for you it is expected to trust in
God and pray to Him as best you can, never to fall into
despair and to struggle according to your strength.*
                                        —Fr. Seraphim Rose

Orthodoxy offers such a rich and varied tradition that it can
overwhelm us. Our good impulse to bring the Church into
our homes can be answered by such a crushing weight of possibilities—long prayer sessions and strict fasting rules, daunting
purchases of prayer books and icons, candles and strange incense
from faraway places. We might see examples of families whose
lifestyles are so transformed by religious practice that we are
unable to imagine it working in our homes—or, to the contrary,
we may see so many Orthodox families whose home lives are
utterly secular that we wonder how much of this practice is really
necessary.

Start slow, ask for help, and follow directions. When we had first considered converting to Orthodoxy, my husband—who had been exploring Orthodoxy for several years—decided to jump right in with both feet. There we were, only the day after a long, tearful conversation about our decision to consider Orthodoxy, and he came into the living room with an icon and candles ready to recite the Canon of St. Andrew. Right there! In our living room!

I came to realize that this kind of zeal and enthusiasm was not all that uncommon among convert families, but at the time I was shocked and struggled to keep my emotions in check. There is just so much that a family could do that it's easy to get carried away and drive each other crazy or damage your relationship. The best advice that I can give is to take things slowly, ask for help, and follow the instructions of your priest as you bring your family towards salvation together. —Amelia, mother of four

Take a deep breath. Start at the beginning.

The two things all Orthodox families should begin doing immediately are very simple: Pray and go to church.

Father Thomas Hopko, of blessed memory, famously quoted his mother's advice regarding the Orthodox spiritual life. Before he was an ordained priest—even before he was a seminarian—the young Thomas was given this maxim as he embarked into the world as a young college student: *Go to church; say your prayers; remember God.* For him, this was an incredibly deep insight on his mother's part. Here, in a few short words, was the fullness of her instruction in the faith. What an acute and discerning statement, both simple and profound, and how empowering to parents who long to see their children grow up to serve Christ and His Church.

When we go to church, we are among the people of God. We partake of the Eucharist and ingest the Body and Blood of Christ, taking Him into our bodies. We are individually transformed into living members of the Body of Christ, and corporately we become that Body and citizens of the Kingdom of God. The priest presents us and our offerings to God and asks that the Holy Spirit descend upon the people and the Gifts and transform them into the Body and Blood of His Son.

> Again we offer unto You this reasonable and bloodless worship, and we ask You, and pray You, and supplicate You: Send down Your Holy Spirit upon us and upon these gifts here offered. And make this bread the precious Body of Your Christ, and that which is in this cup, the precious Blood of Your Christ, making the change by the Holy Spirit. (Epiclesis prayers, Divine Liturgy of St. John Chrysostom)

When we say our prayers, we connect our whole selves in relationship to God. We speak words of adoration, praise, petition, and intercession. We bow and prostrate our bodies to show submission to our Great God and King. We cross ourselves and place the symbol of our redemption over our entire bodies.

When Fr. Thomas spoke of "remembering God," he was very clear that he was talking especially of that practice of the presence of God we discussed earlier. In all our doings, no matter how trivial, we must make an offering of ourselves to God. This can be as simple as crossing ourselves before we get out of bed in the morning or saying prayers before meals. It can mean repeating the Jesus Prayer—Lord, Jesus Christ, have mercy on me, a sinner—with each stroke of the broom on the floor or with each dish we wash. The act of remembering God at all times is transformative and strengthens the walls of our little church.

But where to start?

Begin by saying the Lord's Prayer with your children tonight. Put down the book right now and say it together. We can wait.

Your family just prayed together. Do it before meals; do it before bed; do it before school in the morning. Just one little prayer—which only takes a few seconds to say—and your family has begun the process of establishing the foundations of your little church. Congratulations!

Begin by committing to attendance at every Sunday liturgy, rain or shine, and begin to schedule your extracurricular activities around church. If your family expects you at Mother's Day brunch, tell them you'll hurry over after church. If the soccer team always plays on Sunday morning, let them know that you'll be in church. Make the firm commitment to attend church every Sunday.

From that beginning, all the other ideas in this book can slowly take root.

It is later than you think! Hasten, therefore, to do the work of God. —Fr. Seraphim Rose[11]

Some people love the idea of a fresh clean start and will happily leap into the creation of icon corners and prayer rules with abandon. Others are averse to change and need to slowly and gently work these additions into their homes. Neither approach is wrong. Those who move too fast toy with the danger of burnout, and those who move too slowly risk standing still. However you do it, start here: Pray and go to church.

This book, like Orthodox tradition, contains myriad options and ideas for bringing the faith alive in your home. The more we experience the seamlessness of church life and home life, the more we begin to live in the Kingdom right here on earth. These things can be a blessing to your family if they are added joyfully and prayerfully to your family's rhythm.

We are converts, so we're still kind of formulating this as a family, but this year, we are beginning a new tradition with regard to namedays. We've never kept track of when our namedays were, but we recently discovered that all five of us have our namedays within the same four weeks (which, this year, happens to be during Bright Week). So, we're

going to have a party with church friends on Bright
Saturday, read each saint's life, and provide some
feasting snacks. Eventually, as the kids develop, I'd
like them to share their own saints' stories with our
friends at this party, and perhaps dress up or share
a snack or craft specific to his/her story. —Maura,
mother of three

It is also true, of course, that you will meet many profoundly pious Orthodox people in your lifetime, and many of them will never have done any of this. There are many ways to live a good life, and as long as prayer and a love of Christ and His Church are at the center, one way is not necessarily better than another.

Our tradition is filled with examples of holy people who lived extraordinarily simple lives. We might think of Tolstoy's short story, "The Three Hermits," in which three simple monks lived on a distant island. One day, they were visited by their bishop, who discovered that they didn't even know the Lord's Prayer. He spent his entire visit teaching them the Our Father and then left, satisfied. But as his ship sailed away, he saw the three hermits chasing after him on the water, crying, "Dear Father, we have forgotten the prayer you taught us!" The bishop was amazed to see them walk on water as our Lord did, and asked, "Dear brothers, how do you pray?" They answered, "We say, 'Dear God, there are three of us and there are three of You, have mercy on us!'" The bishop, understanding that they were holier than he and that God had blessed them in their simplicity, said, "Go back to your land and be at peace."

Hold fast to the Church. Read books, specifically about family life or marriage from authors with "Saint" or "Elder" in front of their name. Find couples who are further down that road to glean advice from. Most importantly, pray. Pray hard and often. —Emily, mother of four

Many saints' lives teach us that simple humility and fervent prayer bring us closer to God. Trust in this, and don't get lost in an effort to do everything all at once. Begin to build your little church by laying a foundation of prayer and church attendance, and then build it up layer by layer, a little at a time.

With faith and love, draw near. You have found the greatest gift given, the ability to love and worship the Trinity. Sometimes it's hard, but the rewards are unfathomable.

Ask questions and find a mentor. Sometimes your Godparents/sponsors are great, but other times you may want to look for a family that personifies the qualities you strive for.

You are not an island, but part of a family. Everyone in your family is moving towards the

*same goal, salvation. Some are more collegiate in
their pursuit, others fly by faith alone.*
—*Brooksana, grandmother*

Blessed Fr. Seraphim Rose was once asked in a letter about finding a "true starets" for spiritual guidance. Writing in the 1970s–80s, he was incredulous that such a teacher could be found in the modern world. He offers the following advice to these spiritual seekers, which is good for parents in contemporary society to remember:

1) Learn first of all to be at peace with the spiritual situation which has been given you, and to make the most of it. If your situation is spiritually barren, do not let this discourage you, but work all the harder at what you yourself can do for your spiritual life. It is already something very important to have access to the Sacraments and regular church services. Beyond this you should have regular morning and evening prayers with your family, and spiritual reading—all according to your strength and the possibilities afforded by your circumstances.

2) Among spiritual writings you should read especially those addressed to people living in the world, or which give the ABCs of spiritual life—such as St. John of Kronstadt's *My Life in Christ*, St. Nikodemos' *Unseen Warfare*, the Lives of Saints in general, and Bishop Ignatius Brianchaninov's *The Arena* (this book, while addressed to novices, is suitable for laymen insofar as it gives in general the ABCs of spiritual life as applied to modern times).

3) To help your spiritual growth and remind you of spiritual truths, it would be good to keep a journal (the hardbound record books sold in stationery stores are good), which would include excerpts from the writings of spiritual books which you find

especially valuable or applicable to you, and perhaps comments of your own inspired by reading and reflection, including brief comments on your own shortcomings which you need to correct. St. John of Kronstadt found this especially valuable, as can be seen in his *My Life in Christ*.

4) Don't criticize or judge other people—regard everyone else as an angel, justify their mistakes and weaknesses, and condemn only yourself as the worst sinner. This is step one in any kind of spiritual life.[12]

Many of these things are so much easier for us as parents in the twenty-first century—we have access to the books listed and so many more. With the growth of American Orthodoxy and the increasingly technical advantages that come with living in developing countries, we have access in English to writings of holy men and teachers that before were only to be found in their original languages. But note the deep simplicity of the advice from this holy man: go to church, learn from the fathers, keep a journal, know yourself and your own need for forgiveness and mercy.

Pray with your children, and pray for your children.

Ask God and His saints to help you as you shepherd your family along this path. Pray that all of you will grow in your love for Christ, that each of you will come to yearn for Him and for a life in the Church. This is the most important thing you can do to help your little church grow.

Know also that your family will have its own seasons. There will be seasons of wonderful growth and seasons of rest. There will be seasons when you backslide and regress, and seasons when you wish you could do more but simply cannot. Be patient and pray. Remind yourself that if we were to do everything well, nothing would be a struggle, and we'd be overcome with pride at our accomplishments. There will be hurdles and there will be hardship, and we will grow in humility as we accept and work through them.

Always remember that we fall down and we get back up, and we fall down and we get back up. This is the true rhythm of the Orthodox life.

> My brethren, do all that is in your power not to fall, for the strong athlete should not fall, but, if you do fall, get up again at once, and continue the contest. Even if you fall a thousand times, because of the withdrawal of God's grace, rise up again at each time, and keep on doing so until the day of your death. For it is written: "If a righteous man falls seven times," that is, repeatedly throughout his life, "seven times shall he rise again" [Proverbs 24:16]. —St. John of Karpathos[13]

Don't force children to pray, because that might make them become bitter towards it. Instead, just pray in front of them and ask them to participate. If they refuse to join in, then just pray by yourself and try again the next day. Lead by example.
—Sophia, mother of two

CHAPTER 3

Church Services and Parish Life

Fathers and mothers: Go and lead your child by the hand into the church.

—St. John Chrysostom

Regular attendance at Sunday morning liturgy is a difficult task. Taking time out of busy schedules to honor the feast days is an even loftier goal. Regular Sunday morning liturgy plus twelve (more if you count vigil beforehand) more services throughout the year with children—surely, you jest!

Some of us were less-than-regular before we had children, but becoming parents changes things: We recognize that if we want our children raised in the Church, we're going to have to attend the Church's services. One of the primary messages of this book is that the family is a sacred unit, vital to the life of the Church; it is also the first place our children will learn how to be Christians. Regular attendance and involvement in the Divine Liturgy are crucial.

Liturgy literally means "the work of the people." A priest cannot perform the liturgy alone; the Church—the people—must gather with him. Your family, with their noises and distractions, are part of the people of God, gathered together to do the work of the Liturgy. Saints are not raised outside the Church. We need each other—young and old, children and grandparents—as we do this work of salvation together.

When to Begin

Today.

It can be tempting to postpone taking our children to church until they are "old enough" to behave well. That may sound good, but there are several problems with this strategy:

» First and most importantly, your family will have missed precious years of participation in the Body of Christ and its Sacraments.

» If you have multiple children, you may well wait so long that your oldest has hardly any time left in the church before he or she leaves the household.

» By the time you take your child to church, the experience will be quite unfamiliar and strange, so it will be no surprise if his behavior is poor.

I once worked for a church that thought this way—that keeping the children out of the regular Sunday worship until they were twelve was the best thing for all parties. Children could take part in two hours of Christian programming and education each Sunday from their earliest years (nursery) through the sixth grade. After that, they were expected to be part of the corporate worship service with the grownups. At that point they were expected to sit quietly, fully participate, and be model Christian children. This almost never happened.

It's vitally important for us as parents and as Christian adults in our home parish to communicate through words, actions, and attitudes that the children of the parish (all of them) are full members of the Body of Christ and are welcome at the services of the Church. Yes, children are noisy; yes, children venerate the icons at the wrong time; yes, children sit and talk through the Gospel when everyone should be quiet and paying attention. All of these are true statements, but it doesn't matter. We must develop welcoming, loving attitudes toward the children and young adults of our parishes—not in programs and activities, but in full inclusion. After all, we are joined with them in Christ through Baptism and the Eucharist. There is no separation between adults and children except in terms of how many years we've spent on Earth. Be the loving example, the caring mentor, the welcoming friend to all families. —Caleb

The best way to teach a child how to behave calmly and reverently in church is to bring the child to church. There will be struggles. There will be days when you find you spend as much time outside the nave, walking a fussing child, as you spend inside the services. Just about every parent is at least frustrated with a child's behavior in church on any given Sunday. Yes, every parent. Even the ones whose children look so well-behaved, who stand quietly, gazing serenely around the church—even those parents will tell you they are stressed by their children's behavior.

It can be very easy to simply see church services as a marathon to survive when you have children, or at least, I find myself feeling that way. Because my son is so young, my goal is to have him be comfortable in church; this means that I bring lots of snacks and appropriate church toys (a string of rings for a toy censer, books, etc.), bring him into the narthex when he needs to walk or move around, but also keep him in the narthex to show him what is going on. As he gets older, we'll see what I need to do to help him participate. —Alison, mother of one

Strategies for Struggles

The first preventive move you can make is to help your children develop a worshipful demeanor. When you say your prayers at home, ask them to behave as you'd want them to behave in church: stand, face the icons, pray. Don't fight, don't hit your sister, don't scream. If your child is expected to wear a head-covering in church, wear head-coverings at prayer. Signal to your children that worship in the home and worship in the church are the same—so they require the same kind of attention and respect. Cultivate reverence in this way. It's a slow process, slower for some than others, but it is worthwhile. It's also part of the sacramental element of our attendance in divine services:

> The journey begins when Christians leave their homes and beds. They leave, indeed, their life in this present and concrete world, and whether they have to drive fifteen miles or walk a few blocks, a sacramental act is already taking place, an act which is the very condition of everything else that is to happen. For they are now on their way to constitute the Church, or to be more exact, to be transformed into the Church of God. They have been individuals, some white, some black, some poor, some rich, they have been the 'natural' world and a natural community. And now they have been called to 'come together in one place,' to bring their lives, their very 'world' with them and to be more than what they were; a new community with a new life. We are already far beyond the categories of common worship and prayer. —Alexander Schmemann[14]

Know that there will be a battle before the battle. For most families, it's a struggle just to get to the church. Whether it's one child or eight, getting them cleaned up and dressed and into the car is harder on Sunday than it is on weekday mornings. After that first battle, we arrive, triumphant, in the parking lot, and we brace ourselves, because that was just the warm-up. Next will come the battle inside the church. The kids will squirm or kick or fight, and the parents will struggle.

> *My husband jokes that for years I had a running commentary during the service explaining what was happening, what is coming up, etc. As soon as they were able to help in service and around the church they were given things to do. Be it help with greeting, emptying waste cans, light candles, they were given ownership.* —Jackey, mother of three

As with any battle, victory requires preparation. Many families talk with younger children about good church behavior the night before, after prayers or at bedtime, and again in the car on the way to liturgy. By reminding children what good church demeanor is, we give ourselves a higher chance of success. Our expectations should be clear, and we should always assume the youngest ones need to be reminded and prepared. Try not to badger, nag, or scold. Talk to your child in such a way that you instill the awe and wonder of the liturgy and help prepare him for the joy of meeting God at church.

> *This is such a constant battle.*
> *I think it's about the kids knowing your expectations, and making sure those expectations are developmentally appropriate. For instance, it's*

ridiculous to expect a two-year-old to hold still and stand up the entire service, so building in breaks and milestones ("Look, here comes the Gospel!") is helpful.

The most successful Sundays for us have been the ones that have begun with our preparing the kids beforehand: "We're going to church in an hour. What do we do in church?" "We sing, we pray, and we listen." "Do we hit our sisters?" "No!" "Do we cry because we don't want to do something?" "NO!" "Do we ask nicely and quietly if we have to use the bathroom?" "Yes!" "Do we sing along or do we pout?" "We sing because God likes our singing!" That sort of thing. —Maura, mother of three

There is no quick fix for children's behavior in church. Parents must train their children to behave respectfully and appropriately, and that's a process that takes years. At the same time, parents should also strive to keep their expectations realistic (a two-year-old will not behave as a ten-year-old might) and consistently provide a good and loving example.

There is a temptation to threaten and force a child into submission in church, and surely we've all felt it. The problem is that our goal is not simply to worship in silence, but to worship in love. If we want our children to feel at home in the church, to feel loved and welcomed, we should be loving and welcoming them.

We need to communicate to the children: We want you here, we love you, and we're glad you're here.

> *Lest you think we have got it all together, I have to confess that our children are usually the ones who are causing a ruckus in church. My wife jokes that she didn't hear a sermon in over a year after our first children were born: we spent so much time outside the service! It's exhausting, embarrassing, and frustrating. It's humiliating to carry your screaming toddler bodily from the liturgy because he has—for the third time—thrown the service book at his sibling. But—and I emphasize this here—it's necessary for raising saints to teach our children how to honor the Lord's day and to love and serve their brothers and sisters in Christ during the liturgy. Be creative, be patient, be kind, be loving, and ask for help when the going gets to be too difficult.*
> *—Caleb*

The youngest children may need some small distractions. Many parents will have a little church bag that contains something to keep a toddler's hands busy. Ideally, nothing in the bag should make noise (even when pounded on the floor or seats). You might include little books about the Divine Liturgy or saints' lives, and perhaps paper and pencils to keep their hands busy while they soak in the liturgy. Parents can buy small, inexpensive photo albums and fill them with icon cards so the kids can rearrange and play with icons.

> Children who suffer from boredom in church overcome it more easily if they are not afraid to talk about it. It can be mentioned as a temptation for adults too. (Children see them looking at their watches, or starting to gossip . . .) One can also encourage a child to tell Christ about his own problems and joys during a service if he is tired of following—even to talk to Him about his boredom, and ask God to help him appreciate the service.[15]

Ultimately, however, distractions are not the answer. We need to focus on our goal: Are we just trying to quiet the children down, or are we hoping to raise saints? If our goal is to invite them into the worship and to make them a part of it, then we must do the opposite of distracting them. We must constantly be bringing their attention back to the services.

As we stand in church with our children, we should encourage them to sing. Even the youngest children can hum along to "Lord, have mercy" and sing "Amen!" One- and two-year-olds can sing songs—especially if they hear those songs at home, sung by their parents. Add your church's regular hymns to the lullabies you sing at home, and young children will know the songs.

Some people say not to stress about little children who wander or make noise during church, but I prefer to set boundaries early if possible. The best-behaved kids are the ones we've been strictest

*with. It takes dedication, but if you're willing to
hold your baby/toddler most of the time, and not
set them down for any longer than you can expect
them to stand still during a service, then they won't
need discipline or retraining later when you decide
they're old enough to be expected to stay still.*
—David, father of seven

Little ones, whose attention spans are so short, can be called to notice different parts of the service. Watch in your book and announce, "Here's the doxology—we're singing God's glory! Here comes the Small Entrance, honey, get ready! Father's coming—can you see him? Is he holding the Gospel? Can you see it?" If you communicate excitement to them about each part of the Divine Liturgy, they will learn to recognize the milestones and watch for them. There is always something happening in the liturgy; point it out.

And of course, we are surrounded by icons. We can carry little ones around the church when they get fussy and teach them to venerate the icons. We can whisper the stories of the saints to our children and let them know that everyone in God's Holy Kingdom is together in communion. We can recognize the company of the saints in our church.

Anyone old enough to read will greatly benefit from following along with the service. Let your children experience the service from inside it in this way, and help them to focus on the prayers by following along and by singing. If your parish does not provide service books, check online Orthodox bookstores. There are many service books, and several publishers offer guides to the liturgy written especially for children, with larger print, pictures, and explanations of the meaning behind the liturgy.

Be extremely patient and be flexible when you have young children at church. They are not used to being confined for so long. Set reasonable guidelines so they may take breaks (after every thirty minutes take a water break outside the sanctuary). Teach them how to whisper well. Use hand signals that could be used to ask questions or give directions. Direct them to stand during the main parts of the services: small and big entrance, Gospel, Creed, Hymn to the Theotokos, Our Father, consecration, and communion. Allow them to sit in other parts of the service. Bring with you Orthodox books for them to read. —Yola, mother of three

Parents can develop special rituals for children too—little things we do at different parts of the service to help the kids be part of this worshipping Body of Christ. You might move to different parts of the church at different parts of the service so there is a physical rhythm to the liturgy.

One day, my girls and I were discussing the Gospel reading about the woman with the issue of blood who touched the hem of Christ's garment and was healed. She hadn't spoken or even touched Him directly—she had faith that His power was so great, that touching just the hem of His garment would heal her. I mentioned that some people touch Father's robe during the Great Entrance in hopes of spiritual and physical healing. Since then, when we hear the Cherubic Hymn, my girls take their places on Father's route. As the acolytes pass, they're crossing themselves and lowering their heads, but they're also gearing up and getting ready. When Father passes by, they touch the hem of his garment, and then only after he has returned inside the Royal Doors do they come back to their usual positions. Beautiful little rituals like this involve them prayerfully in the service and give them something to do. It's a little milestone in the service; the ritual busies them for a few moments, and the movement refreshes them. —Elissa

These are great strategies for raising children who love the Church and for training them to be quiet and respectful during the services. But let's be clear: There is no prescription for a perfect experience with perfect children in church. No matter how much we work at creating the ideal liturgical experience, it's going to be a struggle. But we Christians aren't afraid of struggle, are we? That's what this life on Earth is—it's our opportunity to struggle.

Parents must not walk into church with unreasonable expectations. It is unfair and demoralizing to demand perfection from children—perfect attentiveness, perfect obedience, perfect stillness. Indeed, we must be as aware of ourselves as we are of our children. (Taking care of the speck in our own eye, as it were.) Our challenge is to firmly and lovingly guide our children without becoming angry or distracted from our own prayerful liturgical experience.

> *Years ago, a priest told me to imagine a monk whose assignment was to watch the candles in the narthex throughout the services. He keeps the candles in place, burning as they should, but does not let them get out of control. Naturally, the flames flicker and move, sometimes quite dramatically, but he is not concerned. He isn't asked to keep the fire still, but simply to keep its liveliness in check, lest there be damage. My priest suggested I should see my children as candles whose quiet movements and flickerings are, in fact, quite beautiful.* —Elissa

Pride rears up in anger when a child dares to disobey or distract us, but humility defeats pride. We should remind ourselves we're not perfect either. Our own minds wander; we lose focus; we forget to pray. We're not infallible, and just as we ask God to forgive our iniquities and heal our infirmities, we must be even more merciful with children. The irony in this situation is that—because of our infirmity—we are focusing on the failures of our children and failing to recognize our own failure to engage in the liturgy.

It is helpful to remind ourselves that just as we tire of teaching children the same lesson a hundred times, God must get awfully tired of trying to teach us the same things again and again. If we can remember we are weak, like the children placed in our care, then we can pass along to them the mercy and forgiveness God has generously poured down upon us.

> *Don't give up [bringing your children to church].*
> *My children are not quiet children. They move*
> *around and complain and pick on each other*
> *during church. I was never able to get them to sit*
> *quietly with me as I saw other children do. We*
> *spent most of the service moving around. We would*
> *start in the front row, then go outside, move to the*
> *quiet room, go outside, head upstairs, go to the car,*
> *back to the front row, outside, etc. We've had our*
> *fair share of looks and even a few comments from*
> *other parishioners that brought me to tears and*
> *had me running to the car to go home. My skin*

is thicker than it was the first few years of raising kids!

Sometimes (not consistently), I'll have crayons/ pencil and paper for them to use. Lately, they will spend the time drawing saints (as they see them on the icons at church) which is nice.

We kept coming and now a few of my boys serve in the altar. —Amity, mother of four

If we are to show children they are beloved, welcome members of the Body of Christ, we must behave in a loving manner. We must find a way to exude love even as we're trying to get them to stop talking or hitting or throwing—whatever it is, we have to call to them lovingly and engage them lovingly. That's not easy. Paul tells us, "Though I speak with the tongues of men and of angels, but have not love, I have become sounding brass or a clanging cymbal" (1 Cor. 13:1). When I'm standing there in church, angry with a child, if I have not love, they're not going to be learning about the faith from me. If we want them to know God, and if God is love, then we need to be showing them love, especially in church!

Love bears all things, believes all things, hopes all things, endures all things—even the frustrating disobedience of children. Love endures it patiently. If we can endure disobedience while maintaining patience and love and even prayerfulness, then attending this liturgy with our children may be more fruitful for us than attending alone.

Our children will learn how to behave in church by watching

how we behave in church; if we are fighting and angry and demanding, that's what they'll learn. But if we are prayerful and loving and eager to pray and sing and stand for hours, they'll learn to be that way too.

This is not to say that wrong behavior is to be ignored and discipline laid aside simply because we parents are also imperfect people. As usual, it's not just the act of going to church but the example we set that teaches them the most. *Discipline* means "to teach." It has the same root as *disciple* (student). Vengeful punishment of our children for misbehavior is not teaching them how to behave and how to worship during the liturgy. It's a fine line all parents must walk as we strive to do the work of parenting through the services: focusing our children, focusing our own attention, modeling right behavior, and correcting missteps along the way.

Church Is Not Just for Sunday

Take a moment to add your parish's calendar of services to your own calendar, and don't assume that it's best to bring your children only to Sunday services. Indeed, the hustle and bustle of a full Sunday liturgy is often more overstimulating to children (and their parents) than the more peaceful weekday services. If you can, take advantage of weekday liturgies and any Vespers or Paraklesis services your parish might offer. You may be surprised to find that some of the additional services are actually more family-friendly than Sunday liturgy.

More importantly, coming to church more than once a week will integrate worship into your daily life. It's an antidote to our modern problem of having separated our church lives from our daily lives, bringing church into the everyday.

On my first visit to an Orthodox monastery, Papa Yousif gave us a tour of the grounds, finishing in the beautiful Katholikon. As we admired the carved iconostasis, sudden shrieks burst forth. I was horrified to see my girls running and squealing around the church as if they were on a playground. I hastened to scold them, but Papa Yousif stopped me and reminded me to be grateful that they know they're in their Father's house. I often think of that day and pray that my children will always feel the Church is truly their loving home. —Elissa

Parish life

There is more to raising children in a parish than simply attending services. Becoming a part of the community brings challenges and blessings, and it will ultimately provide you and your children with the opportunity to grow as true members of the Body of Christ.

FIND A WAY TO VOLUNTEER IN THE PARISH

Most parishes need help, but that's not the main reason you should volunteer. Truly, when you do the work, you will begin to feel real membership in the parish. Families with small children can help in the parish. One parent can teach Sunday school while the other watches the baby, or you can bring a dish to a coffee hour potluck, or help clean the church at some point during the week. If you can sing, join the choir. You don't have to say yes to every request, but do find your place in the parish.

MAKE FRIENDS WITH OTHER FAMILIES IN THE PARISH

If there are other parents with children around the same age as yours, it is well worth the effort to get to know them. Even if you don't share the same opinions on many things, over time you will find that having Orthodoxy in common creates a bond and that it's a blessing to have another Orthodox parent around.

Make intergenerational friends. Befriend the lonely college students and the old men; get to know everyone in Christ's Church, and always remember that the little yiayias and babushki have likely raised children of their own, and they may be willing to share wise advice if you're willing to listen.

We must always remember that the Church is a spiritual hospital—Christ came to heal the sinners, and we are all collected here in our sinfulness and imperfection. We are patients in the spiritual hospital—children, adults, babies, clergy—so we should expect to see some sickness and weakness in the people who surround us.

In *The Screwtape Letters*, C. S. Lewis looks at the spiritual struggle from the other side, from the perspective of the demons who work to keep their "patients" from salvation. In a passage that might help us as we struggle in our own parish lives, a demon reflects on how easily tempted we are by the unattractiveness of the parishioners who surround us:

> When he gets to his pew and looks round him he sees just that selection of his neighbors whom he has hitherto avoided. You want to lean pretty heavily on those neighbors. Make his mind

flit to and fro between an expression like 'the body of Christ' and the actual faces in the next pew. It matters very little, of course, what kind of people that next pew really contains. You may know one of them to be a great warrior on the Enemy's side. No matter. Your patient, thanks to Our Father Below, is a fool. Provided that any of those neighbors sing out of tune, or have boots that squeak, or double chins, or odd clothes, the patient will quite easily believe that their religion must therefore be somehow ridiculous.[16]

Try to resist the inevitable urge to compare yourself and your family to the other people in your parish. Know that the family that seems to be effortlessly perfect is likely struggling in ways you can't see, and the family that seems to be a mess may in fact have a more profound piety than you would imagine. God knows our hearts, and we are here to support and love one another along the journey.

Inviting the Priest into Your Home

Parish life is not just about taking your family to church; it's also about inviting your priest to bring the Church into your home.

HOUSE BLESSINGS

In January, the Church celebrates the Great Feast of Theophany, the day on which Jesus Christ was baptized by John the Forerunner in the Jordan River. As Christ sanctified the waters with His presence, priests all over the world will bless the waters of the Earth. At church that week, you will be given at least one bottle of holy water to take home. Place it in your prayer corner.

In most Orthodox traditions, a period of house blessings

immediately follows. From Theophany through the beginning of Great Lent, the parish priests will travel from home to home, blessing each family's house or apartment. This is a wonderful opportunity not only to have your little church sanctified, but for your children to spend some time with your priest and to make lasting memories of being splashed with holy water while singing joyful hymns through every room of the home.

To have your house blessed, first ask your priest how to be placed on his blessing schedule. This can be simple in smaller parishes or more complex in larger parishes. Take a few moments to discuss the process with him, as this varies widely. Ask your priest about his preferences, but know that there is no wrong way to have your house blessed. Following are some questions you'll want to ask your priest.

What items do I need to supply?

Generally speaking, you'll want to have a candle and a bowl for holy water handy. Prepare a list of the living members of this household, as the priest will want to list them in intercessory prayers and blessings during the service. You may be asked to provide your bottle of holy water, although some priests carry holy water with them. In Slavic traditions, the priests carry a little whisk which they'll use to sprinkle the water, while others might use a *randistirion*, and still others will suggest you provide a bouquet made of fresh basil or rosemary. Find out what your priest prefers.

Does the priest prefer to stay for dinner?

In a smaller parish, priests often come to bless your home and to spend an evening with the family, joining you for dinner (if you graciously invite him). Other priests shepherd large parishes and have to bless several homes every day. Ask him if he will be pressed for time, preferring just a short blessing and no meal. Note that Orthodox priests are famously plied with food throughout this period, and in the interest of being gracious they are sometimes forced to accept multiple dinner offers in a single day. Check in with your priest to find out what would be most convenient and appropriate in his circumstances.

Should I pay the priest?
Ask whether it is customary to give a monetary gift, and try to be aware of your priest's circumstances. In some jurisdictions, especially in those where stewardship and tithing have not yet caught on, it is customary to offer the priest a gift of money (to cover his fuel costs and expenses and to help him if he is impoverished as are so many priests). In other jurisdictions, priests cannot accept your money and may be uncomfortable with the offer. Remember, we don't pay for sacraments. Any monetary offering is just that—an offering from your treasury of your own free will. Father will bless your house without money as well.

It is nice to check in with your priest to understand his expectations and preferences, but there truly is no wrong way to have your house blessed.

Many people will become very stressed about cleaning their homes before a house blessing—after all, their priest is about to walk through every room in the house. Know that priests are not judging your home, and they don't mind stepping over toys. Certainly, leaving out the dirty laundry could get awkward, but there is no need to cause yourself and your family undue stress. On the one hand, it is hospitable to take the time to clean up, but on the other, there is something humble about allowing a priest to come in and "bless your mess." Don't ever let your messy house stop you from inviting your priest inside.

Slava

The wonderful Serbian tradition of *Krsna Slava* is beginning to take root in some American homes. Serbian families celebrate the day on which their ancestors were first baptized into the Church by taking the saint celebrated on that day as their patron saint. Every year on this feast day, the family gathers with close friends and god-family, and the priest comes to bless a specially made loaf of bread called the *slavski kolache* in a beautiful prayer service.

Many American families, like the Serbian families so many hundreds of years ago, are converting to Orthodoxy for the first time, and some have chosen to mark the date of their entry into the Church by claiming a Slava. This family feast day becomes a beautiful occasion to gather with loved ones and offer up prayers of thanksgiving, celebrating the feast of a beloved saint.

If you would like your priest to come serve a Slava in your home, note that if he's not from the Serbian jurisdiction, he will need a Serbian *Book of Needs*, or you can find the Slava service online. Ask your priest what you'll need, but expect the following:

> » **Kolache:** Bake a round loaf of bread (it's okay to use a mix you buy in the store, and to mix the dough in a breadmaker or mixer). When the dough is ready, pinch off about a quarter of it and set it aside, and place the rest in a greased round

pan. Use the extra dough to create an attractive design, and attach it to the loaf by brushing a layer of egg white like glue. Some very talented bakers make beautiful designs on their bread, including vines and grapes and icons, but some others—like those in the Bjeletich family—simply braid some dough and lay it out in a cross on top of the loaf. Bake as the recipe directs.

» **Kolache cloth or napkin and a bread knife:** Place a napkin or cloth atop the kolache so the priest can set it on the floor to catch crumbs of the blessed bread when he cuts it.

» **Wine:** Open a bottle of wine for the blessing. You can finish the wine at dinner.

» **Zhito or wheat:** Families also prepare some boiled wheat, which is identical to *koliva* except that the wheat is not offered in memorial but is also blessed in the Slava service.

» **Candle:** Place a new candle on your prayer corner, which the priest will light in the service and which can burn in the center of the dinner table throughout the celebration.

» **Family list:** Prepare a list of the members of the household, both those living and those who have departed this life, as the priest will want to pray for them during the service.

» **Dinner:** The Slava prayers are traditionally followed by a joyful dinner shared with the priest, his family, and your loved ones.

Hospital Visits & Special Blessings

Look up your priest's cell phone number and program it into your phones. Whenever someone is in the hospital, perhaps during illness or injury or when delivering a child, let your priest know.

One of the wonderful functions of a priest is to visit you during those critical times, to support you through joy, struggle, and sorrow.

Many families do not call on their priest for assistance, not understanding that there are special prayers and blessings he can offer. When we do call on our priest, we come to understand that along with powerful prayers, he brings comfort and reassurance, making the Church present at these most important moments.

BABIES

When a baby is born, let your priest know right away. He can come and read beautiful Orthodox prayers at the naming of the baby on the eighth day. In some traditions, because the mother has co-created life with God, she is considered too holy to mix with the regular folk at church and remains home for forty days. This coincides nicely with the modern medical recommendation to keep newborns away from the public for six weeks; we might say the wisdom of the Church understood this all along.

When the forty days are completed, arrange for a churching. Mother and child will arrive at the church for the first time since the birth, and the priest will have special blessings for both of them before they enter the sanctuary. In most traditions, the priest will carry the child up to the iconostasis and present him or her, mirroring Christ's own presentation in the Temple. (In some parishes, this may be done along with the naming on the eighth day.)

A child can be baptized after forty days (indeed, the prayers of the churching are actually the beginning of the baptismal service). There is no need to wait months or years before baptizing your child, and in fact, many babies fuss and cry less if they are baptized younger. Again, ask your priest what you should bring to the service, as this varies in the different Orthodox traditions. In most cases, the godparents will supply a cross on a chain and perhaps a white garment—though in some cases, the parents supply the garment. Be clear and ask. You'll need to supply a candle; people often like to tie a beautiful ribbon around it. In the Greek church, you will probably also bring olive oil and soap, and often parents will supply a pin—a little ribbon with a cross on it—for guests to wear to commemorate the momentous occasion.

Choosing godparents can be difficult, and often the extended family has strong opinions. Select someone you feel will truly shepherd your child in the faith, who is trustworthy and a good example to your child. Ultimately, this decision belongs in the hands of the parents and should reflect careful, prayerful consideration. It is a great blessing for children to have another trusted adult to whom they can turn with questions or worries, and the right godparents can be an important loving presence in your child's life.

In most traditionally Orthodox societies, the godparents become like family. By selecting loving godparents for your children, we bring the Church into our family structure in a profound way. Recall that godparents fill a vital role in connecting the child with the Church throughout life. Choose people whose example will make a lasting impression on your child's spiritual development; select members of your parish who will be there to help you out when times are troublesome. Above all, choose godparents whose love of Christ is clear and will be a pattern for your child to follow throughout her life.

Your parish is another family—consecrated by God to help you come to salvation. You are as important as the oldest baba and the youngest child. Your involvement in the life of the Church will bless and sanctify that community as the Holy Spirit works through you to bring the presence of Christ into every relationship. Don't be afraid of "ruining" the parish by misbehaviors and mishaps. Go to serve, go to grow, go to love, go to learn. Your children will learn from you to form a lasting relationship with their future parish community, and their faith will be the stronger for it.

CHAPTER 4

Creating Sacred Space

It's common practice in Orthodox homes to have a special place set aside for family prayer and devotion—a family altar or icon corner used for keeping safe and displaying sacred books and images.

Setting up an icon corner is a crucial part of building your little church. Just as our church buildings are elaborately adorned with images of Christ, His Mother, and the saints, our homes reproduce this in small scale with a family icon corner. There are many ways you can set up your family altar, so what follows is simply a guideline. Your family's altar will include at least an icon or two and may grow to include candles, incense, holy water, holy oils, and vigil lamps.

For those of us who are converts from Protestantism and have grown up with an aversion to images of Christ and the saints, setting up the first icon corner can come with a mixture of fear and embarrassment. I remember the first time a family of

*Protestant friends came to our home and saw our
icon corner placed in a prominent location. It was
incredibly uncomfortable. The thing to remember
is that everybody comes to Christ differently. Your
experience of icons and praying with them will
be different from that of most people you meet.
Remember you were once shy of images and maybe
even hostile to those who loved and venerated
icons. Don't let embarrassment stop you from setting up this small piece of your parish life at home.*
—Caleb

Location

Ideally, our church temples face east, toward the rising sun. A
simple way to recreate the temple at home is to place your family
icon corner on an eastern wall so that your family will be facing
east during prayer times. For some people, that may be easier said
than done. If you can't place it on an eastern wall for whatever
reason, the next best choice is to place your icons on a prominent
wall in a central living area. Children often have a smaller icon
area in their bedrooms with their patron saints, a cross, and an
icon of Christ and the Theotokos.

The methods of displaying icons are as varied as people's styles
and tastes. Some families use bookshelves or specialty corner
shelves and cabinets; others simply begin by hanging an icon on
the wall.

In our house, the icon corner is anchored by a small shelf placed vertically in the corner of the living room. The shelf already had three dividing sections, and those little dividers became three small shelves for smaller-sized icons, candles, holy oil, and palms from Palm Sunday. Surrounding our icons is a collection of larger and medium-sized icons which have been given to the family as gifts. We have St. George slaying the dragon, St. Xenia the Fool for Christ of St. Petersburg, St. Seraphim of Sarov, St. Herman of Alaska, and Ss. Vladimir and Olga. Above our icon corner is an icon of the "Not Made by Hands" variety printed on fabric. Each of these icons has taken on a special meaning in our family and is an anchor to our daily life. The icon corner overlooks all our daily activities of fun and play. —Caleb

Icon corners often grow over time as the family brings various holy items home to this special space, filling it with meaningful and useful items. Each family will bring their own flavor to the icon corner, and no two will be exactly alike. What all family altars have in common is that they are the gathering place for prayer and worship in the daily rhythm of life. There isn't a wrong way to set up your icon corner. The only question to answer is what your particular altar will look like as you begin.

Whom Do You Know?

Which icons you place on your family altar is a personal decision. Ours have stayed mostly the same through the years, but we've had visitors stop by and new residents move in on occasion. There are few hard and fast rules when it comes to the icons in your icon corner, so don't get too caught up on who should be there; rather, focus on who is there. It's not uncommon to include icons of all the family patrons in the central icon corner. Others will place the icons of family patrons in the bedrooms and not as part of the main altar. You can't have the wrong icons, and you can't put your icons in the wrong place.

> *I have a bookcase. The top has candle, prayer books, Bibles, some relics, and a blessing cross. Icons are arranged with Christ in the center, the Theotokos and St. John of Kronstadt on the left; St. John the Forerunner and St. Nicholas on the right; our family patron saints under those. On one wall we have put icons for our boys at their height.*
> —Jared, father of three

Depending on your background, there may be special saints specific to your country of origin, parish, or jurisdiction. These can be an excellent addition to your family icon corner. If you attend a parish dedicated to a particular saint or feast day, seek out that icon for your family altar and create another connection between your home and parish. If your country of origin has a connection to a particular saint, invite him into your home by finding his icon. If you've developed a personal devotion to a special saint, bring her into your home through her holy icon.

Begin with two icons: Christ and the Theotokos. If all you have is a cross, that's a good starting place, too. Don't wait until you have everything together before you start to pray. Place your icons in a prominent location. If you have the icons of Christ and His Mother, place Our Lord on the right and Our Lady on the left (just like at church), and your cross in the middle between them. If you only have one icon, place it in a conspicuous location in your house and use it for prayer. If you have no printed icons, you have your children and your spouse to pray with you—the living icons of Christ in your life!

We have two—one upstairs and one downstairs in the dining room. We use the one upstairs for morning and evening prayers because of its proximity to the bedrooms, and any special things (i.e., house blessing prayers, mealtime prayers, moms gathering to say an akathist for our kids) are done at the corner downstairs.

We decided to do it this way because we kept finding ourselves halfway through the kids' bedtime routine upstairs, and getting all the kids downstairs again, and then getting all the kids back up one more time was prohibitive. We were more likely to

pray if there was always an accessible space for it.
Upstairs, we have icons of all our patron saints,
plus Christ, the Theotokos, St. Nicholas (our
unofficial family patron), and the icon of Thomas's
belief. Downstairs is more simple—Christ, the The-
otokos, patrons for me and my husband, and an
icon of Christ and the children. —Maura, mother
of three

Step by Step

Locate an east wall or eastern corner of your house or apartment.
If none exists that is convenient for prayer, then select the most
convenient place in your living area.

Place icons where they can be seen and venerated. Some people like to use a bookshelf or small chest of drawers where other
holy objects (oils, incense, the Bible, prayer books) can be kept.

Arrange your icons in a way that is aesthetically pleasing to
you. Start by placing icons of Christ and His Mother central to
the other icons, with Christ on the right side and the Theotokos
on the left.

Some families intentionally place icons low enough for very
young children to venerate, which is a beautiful idea, but only if
you don't mind the icon being picked up and carried around. If
you want the icons to stay in the family icon corner, then make
sure the low ones are secure enough on the wall that they can't
become weapons in the hands of zealous toddlers.

Miracles happen through the prayers of small children. Whatever they ask of God He gives them because they are guileless
and He hears their pure prayer. I remember one time our parents
had gone out into the field and had left me in the house with
my two younger siblings. The sky suddenly darkened and a
torrential rainstorm began. "What will our parents do now?," we
said. "How will they get back home?" The two little ones began
crying. "Come here," I told them, "we will ask Christ to stop the
rain." The three of us knelt down before the family's icons and
prayed. In just a few minutes the rain stopped. —Elder Paisios[17]

The icons you select to place before your children will leave an
impression on them. Many who grew up in Orthodox homes
grew to fear the icons because the images were so stern or
because their parents didn't introduce them to the saints depicted
and make them real in their family. Other children grow up with
a profound love of icons and the saints depicted. Perhaps an icon
of the Theotokos snuggling baby Jesus reminds them of the love
God has for them. Maybe seeing the brave St. George slay the
dragon becomes a source of security and courage in the face of
nightmares. Don't be afraid of placing holy images before children and teaching them to reverence the icons with love and to
see the saints depicted as living members of the Body of Christ
who care and pray for them.

*When we began, our prayer corner was one icon
hanging on a wall. Over the years, it has grown to
include icons of various beloved saints. When we*

*added candlelight to our prayers, we brought in
a console table to hold the candles. Soon, it was
filled with a censer, holy water, and various bottles
of holy oils given to us when our children were sick.
A shelf below holds Bibles and religious children's
books and prayer books, while the drawers are filled
with prayer lists and incense, extra candles and
printed prayers. Now several icons hang above
the table, carefully arranged, with Christ and the
Theotokos surrounded by saints chosen by the
family. To the right of the icons hangs a white
plate, separated into sections for "the sick and the
suffering" and "those who have died in the hope of
the resurrection," on which the family writes names
with a dry-erase marker. There is also a wide clear-
glass vase, filled to the brim with blessed palm
crosses and flowers collected at feast days. —Elissa*

Playing with Fire: Of Candles and Incense

Another element to creating sacred space in your little church is
the inclusion of candles and incense on your family altar. These
can be powerful additions to your regular prayer rule. Lighting
candles and burning incense also help to shore up the notion
that we are bringing the parish into our own home and that our
houses are places where Christ and His angels and saints are
welcome.

*We keep a prayer table and bench in the entryway
of our home. This is symbolic for many reasons. It
is the first thing that is seen when you enter in our
front door. It is where we gather for family prayer
each night. We keep our family Bible and other
meaningful items (though we don't have any icons
yet) on and around this table which is really a cabinet. Inside, all of the Baptismal candles, rosaries,
saint dolls, etc. We chose to centralize all of our
spiritual items here to make the statement that
this space is special and requires reverence. It helps
family prayer time go smoothly because they know
it's set apart.* —Melanie, mother of five

CANDLES

The candles lit before icons of the saints reflect their ardent love
for God for Whose sake they gave up everything that man prizes
in life, including their very lives, as did the holy apostles, martyrs
and others. These candles also mean that these saints are lamps
burning for us and providing light for us by their own saintly living, their virtues and their ardent intercession for us before God
through their constant prayers by day and night. The burning
candles also stand for our ardent zeal and the sincere sacrifice we
make out of reverence and gratitude to them for their solicitude
on our behalf before God. —St. John of Kronstadt[18]

Candles are ubiquitous in today's culture, and so finding candles
shouldn't be hard. Some families will purchase extra candles at

church and burn them at home so they have the sweet, clean burning of beeswax. Others will purchase votive or tealight candles in bulk and keep them handy for any occasion. You cannot burn the wrong kind of candle. Find the style that suits your family's needs and budget. All candles can represent the light of Christ in our lives and will aid your prayer times.

> *My sacred space is a traditional old believer icon corner. Just a few icons and a cross. And every one in the house has an icon corner in their rooms. In the child's just one icon and an oil lamp. Always an icon with a good story behind it that she could read about.* —Stephen, father of one

Light candles during family prayer times. If safety allows, have your little ones blow the candles out at the end of each family prayer session.

Light candles in front of a particularly special icon or important saint whose intercession you are seeking. There is no wrong time to use candles, and in fact the candle itself can act in two important ways. It can both remind you to pray and stand as a lasting memorial to your prayer as you go about the day. Just because you've left your icon corner does not mean your prayers have ceased, and your lit candle can serve as your prayer's continued presence before God even if your body is absent and your mind is occupied.

*When my grandmother was in the hospital, I kept
a candle lit in front of an icon of St. Panteleimon
throughout the day. When the candle burned out, I
replaced it. I kept this burning for the weeks before
she came home. The day she died, I lit a candle
near an icon of St. Ruth (her namesake) during her
forty days.* —Caleb

INCENSE

Burning incense can be a little trickier. It's tempting to go to the local novelty shop and pick up a few sticks of incense for pennies on the package, but let us encourage you to spend your money better elsewhere. An incense starter kit from an Orthodox supplier, your parish bookstore, or a local monastery is easy to come by and will provide you with more than enough to get you started using incense as part of your prayer discipline.

Assuming you have everything you need, let's take the incense process step by step:

» Gather your supplies: hand censer, charcoal, incense, tongs, lighter.
» For home use, a quarter or eighth of the charcoal disc will be plenty. Break off a piece of the charcoal and hold with tongs over the sink or fire-safe area. Self-lighting charcoal is coated with an incendiary and can catch fire fairly quickly. You definitely don't want to be holding this with your hands when it decides to light.

» Place charcoal wedge in your censer and let sit a few minutes (five or so).

» Add one to three grains of incense to your censer and shake it about to start the burning.

» Once the fragrant smoke begins to waft out of the censer, make the sign of the cross with your censer in front of the icons, then in front of every person in your family (children really appreciate this special blessing).

» Proceed through the house room by room, making sure to bless beds and personal icons, making the sign of the cross in each room.

» After your house is blessed, let the charcoal burn out in a safe place.

This is an activity that can happen any time in an Orthodox home. Special family days (birthdays, name days or slava, anniversaries) are a great time for a family to bless each other and their homes. There are also times when you may feel the desire to burn incense to help freshen the air and clear your thinking. Indeed, recent research from Johns Hopkins University and the Hebrew University in Jerusalem found that burning frankincense activates ion channels in the brain to alleviate anxiety and depression. We should not underestimate the blessings of this ancient Orthodox practice.

We have Jesus and the Theotokos in the center, a cross below them and the icon of the resurrection above them. Fanning off to the sides we have our

family icons, the icons of saints dear to us and an
icon for our church. We have the icons on kissing
level so the kids' icons are lower than the adults'. —
Syra, mother of six

Holy Water

Most Orthodox families will receive holy water once or twice a year to bring home. St. John Maximovitch recommended getting enough to last you the whole year and making sure you drink some every chance you get.

We had a half-size rolltop desk that wouldn't fit
a computer and became a drop point for a lot
of junk. One day, after finding my two-year-old
drinking oil from our vigil lamp, I had a stroke
of genius. I moved the desk into the icon corner.
We now house all of our church and prayer items
(charcoal, incense, candles, jars of candle stubs,
matches, extra oil, wicks, etc.) inside the desk with
the top rolled down. Icons are on the walls, only
a cross, vigil lamp and our dish of sand for our
candles is out in the open. It is too high for even
a toddler with a chair to reach. I was ready to
put the vigil lamp away until the kids were older,
lest I have a Molotov cocktail at the ready. I'm

very thankful we have found a solution. —*Emily,*
mother of three

One beautiful pious practice is to take three sips of holy water (for the Holy Trinity) after your morning prayers with a piece of antidoron from the previous Sunday's liturgy. Many families will offer their children a little holy water whenever the child is nervous or needs to gird herself for something important, like an exam. When you move into a new home that has not yet been blessed by your priest, it's a nice idea to walk through the house and splash a bit in each room, to sanctify your new family space. This is appropriate for lay persons to do before a priest arrives.

The prayer at the blessing of holy water includes a list of its uses:

> For those who draw from it and take from it for the sanctification of their homes . . .
>
> For it to be for cleansing of souls and bodies for all those who draw from it with faith and who partake of it . . .
>
> That all who draw from it and partake of it may have it for cleansing of souls and bodies, for healing of passions, for sanctification of homes, for every suitable purpose . . . (The Service of the Great Blessing of the Water)

MEDICINAL PURPOSES
Keep a small dosage cup (like those that come with medicine bottles) with your holy water and give it to your kids on those nights when they feel poorly but don't require medication.

This was a particularly effective method of "giving medicine" to our girls when they weren't actually sick but were feeling anxious or nervous. Children may ask for medicine when they don't really need it, and this is a way of giving them something good for body and soul—especially for the nervous or anxious person. We would fill a medicine cup or syringe with holy water and have them take a little bit of "medicine," which satisfied their "need" for medicine without putting them in danger. —Caleb

When my daughter Stefanja was born, a dear Serbian priest gave me a little squirt bottle of holy water for her baths, encouraging me to add a few drops to every bath and then to dispose of the bath water in my yard. We found the process of quietly sanctifying each bath made that first year of infancy even sweeter. —Elissa

Holy Oil

The procurement of holy oil may take a little bit of searching. Some parishes distribute holy oil once a year. Many monasteries and churches will be willing to send a small vial of holy oil from a special lampada, a myrrh-streaming icon, or myrrh-streaming relics. A little bit of research and a friendly letter will usually yield a pretty good supply of holy oils to have on hand in your icon corner.

I went on a search for holy oil during a time when our family was experiencing a lot of illness and anxiety over the future. I found that a regular internet search was not as helpful as speaking with other Orthodox about where they had found their oils. I wrote a note to the brothers at St. Nektarios Monastery in Roscoe, New York, asking for oils because my godmother told me she had received some from them. Virgin Mary Joy of All Who Sorrow Cathedral in San Francisco, California, has an internet request form for oil from the lampada near St. John Maximovitch's relics. St. Tikhon's Monastery in South Canaan, Pennsylvania, has myrrh from a streaming icon of St. Anna; and Holy Theotokos of Iveron Russian Orthodox Church in Honolulu, Hawaii, supplies a small amount of myrrh from their wonderworking icon of the Theotokos. I even went so far as to contact the cathedral in Barre, Italy, to ask for myrrh from St. Nicholas's relics, which they gave in abundance. —Caleb

As with holy water, feel free to use holy oil as the need arises. Some Orthodox families will use holy oil with every prayer time.

Others will save it for special occasions of concern or illness.

To use: Place a little of the oil on your finger and make the sign of the cross on the forehead of the person being blessed. This can be a very powerful and emotional experience for parents and their children. Don't hurry. Pray for each person and sign their head with a cross in the name of the Trinity. You may find your children crave this special connection between the two of you and the saint to whom you are praying.

Vigil Lamp

Vigil lamps can be purchased or make a great DIY project for parents and older kids. These can be freestanding or mounted to a wall, hanging over the icons in your icon corner. This may not be something you want to jump right into, depending on your family's situation. Families with small children or living in tight spaces may prefer not to include vigil lamps. Some families may live in apartments or other residences that have restrictions on open flames, regardless of how secure you make your lamp. If you can't use a lamp because of your circumstances, you don't have to. If you do have the ability to hang a vigil lamp near a beloved icon or to place it in a safe spot, this simple act of devotion can be a powerful witness to the family of the light of Christ burning in their hearts.

Vigil lamps are kept burning with a wick floating in olive oil. The gentle light of an oil lamp is aesthetically pleasing and requires very little attention. The oil is inexpensive, and the wicks can be purchased in bulk. These wicks will need to be trimmed regularly and the level of oil kept up, but the lamp will burn with a clean light and doesn't have the danger of hot wax or other problems associated with candles.

In historically Orthodox countries, the oil from the lampada is used as holy oil to bless members of the family. Indeed, most holy oil you might receive is simply the olive oil from a vigil lamp used at a holy site, such as the oil from the lamp that is placed near the relics of St. John Maximovitch in the Russian Orthodox cathedral in San Francisco.

Elder Paisios told an amusing story about the use of holy oil in the home:

> When I lived in the Stomiou Monastery in Konitsa, a field keeper from a neighboring village used to come every Saturday for the evening service at the monastery. The man, who had many children, always asked me to let him light the lampadas in the temple. I allowed him overlooking the fact that he would always spill oil. When he would leave the monastery, he, having walked a while, would fire his shotgun. This always puzzled me, and once I secretly followed him. Having lit the lampadas, he oiled his gun with the oil from the lampada hanging in front of the icon of the Mother of God and, kneeling before it, he asked Her for a little bit of meat for his children. When he left the monastery, a wild nanny-goat was waiting for him with her head bowed. He made one shot, killed the goat and that way he got meat for his children. This was how the Mother of God, listening to his simple prayer, would give him the best meat for his very large family.[19]

If you are earnest and prayerful, there is hardly a wrong way to use holy oil.

As you set out to create sacred space in your home, know that you cannot do this wrong. Set aside a space in your home and let your icon corner develop as it suits your family best. The important thing is to gather together in prayer and to make room in your home to live out your faith. This is an important step in the creation of your little church, and you will continue to return to these sanctifying activities again and again with your children as you grow together in faith.

CHAPTER 5

Developing Your Rhythm

*When your children are still small, you have to help
them understand what is good. That is the deepest
meaning of life.*

—Elder Paisios

Whether they know it or not, every family has its own
rhythm, a routine.

As young single people, our routines are determined by our
school or work schedules and the various social activities, hobbies, and family commitments that shape our days. When for the
first time we become parents, that routine is dramatically altered:
the household's schedule suddenly revolves around the baby's eating and sleeping cycles.

As the child grows, the parents begin to intentionally establish a routine: mornings begin with tooth-brushing and getting
dressed and breakfast, days end with baths and goodnight stories.
We understand that young children benefit from a regular routine, but what we often forget is that all human beings benefit
from a healthy rhythm.

Families in the United States often struggle with schedules

that grow increasingly out of control as their children grow older. In an effort to produce wholesome and well-rounded children, American parents want to offer them opportunities to explore their artistic side, to excel in athletics, and to attain a high level of socialization. As a result, children are involved in multiple extra-curricular leagues and events, and each of those places demands on the family schedule. Eventually, the routine is determined not by the parents' good judgment but by the demands of coaches and teachers who cannot consider the overall well-being of each indi-vidual household. This results in an overly hectic, fragmented, and exhausting day-to-day life.

> Everything in this life passes away—only God remains, only He is worth struggling towards. We have a choice: to follow the way of this world, of the society that surrounds us, and thereby find ourselves outside of God; or to choose the way of life, to choose God Who calls us and for Whom our heart is searching. —Fr. Seraphim Rose[20]

Making Time for Prayer

Making time for prayer can be one of the greatest struggles for families. There are so many other activities pulling and fighting for our attention that adding one more thing can be overwhelm-ing. Between sports practice, weekly church service, full-time jobs, driver's ed, and ballet class, it can be hard enough for a fam-ily to eat a meal together, let alone say a full prayer rule. What with all the expected elements of a pious Orthodox family life, it can be so easy to just chuck it all out in the name of preserving our sanity.

We pray before our meals, after our meals and
sometimes a short prayer in the morning. —*Syra,*
mother of six

When the Orthodox claim that we have the "fullness of the faith," we are referring to more than our apostolic succession and aversion to change. Our faith has fullness because it is therapeutic: it heals us, bringing us back to a wholesomeness in Christ, in which we are spiritually, physically, and mentally well.

The Church in her wisdom offers us a healthy rhythm that leads us to a wholesome and good routine. Instead of the frantic pace of a family spinning out of control, the Church provides an intentional, peaceful rhythm that is firmly grounded in prayer and love. In an Orthodox home, time is put to holy use so that the routine is not tearing us apart and wearing us out, but actually contributes to our spiritual lives. When we sanctify time with prayer rules, liturgical cycles, and spiritual seasons, we use time itself as it was intended: as a reminder of God and a tool for our spiritual growth.

[We pray at] meals and toddler evening prayers.
Occasionally parent evening prayers, too. —*Peter,*
father of one

God exists in eternity and is not bound by time, and yet He has given us time as a gift so that we might use it to order our lives.

We should not be slaves to time but should think of ourselves as stewards of time; we use it wisely or waste it. At the Creation, God set aside time for His newly formed creatures to rest; at Mt. Sinai, the wandering Israelites were commanded to set aside and consecrate a day wholly to God; and in Leviticus, the Sabbath commandments extended to years dedicated to rest and festival as the people celebrated God's presence—even the land was given rest from the labor of producing a harvest. This liturgical rhythm is built into the fabric of Scripture, and Christ Himself calls us to set aside heavy burdens and to follow Him.

Given the gift of time by God, parents become the gatekeepers of the family's rhythm. We should not allow outside forces to dictate our rhythm, but instead carefully consider each schedule obligation and simply say no when an activity encroaches on our family's well-being.

Proper stewardship requires that we take a good look at our family's schedule and priorities. If parents sit down with a weekly calendar and really look at the time being spent on the essential activities like school, they may find a large portion of their time is being directed toward things like television, movies, or staring blankly at phones or tablets, doing goodness knows what on the internet in our private corner of the house.

When the parents sit down and map out their family's routine, reflecting on what actually happens in their day (as opposed to what should happen on the best of days), they can analyze their routine and identify the items that need to be removed or altered. Just as we work out our financial budgets, we must budget our most precious commodity, time.

Take some time now to go over your weekly time budget

together with your spouse. Identify those gaps of time each day when everyone is usually present (barring unforeseen events) and establish those few minutes for family prayer.

Consider the following schedule used by the Shoe-maker family:

6:00 am   Mom and Dad wake up, shower, say
personal prayers

6:30 am   Kids wake up, family eats breakfast

6:45 am   Kids dress and family says morning
prayers

7:00 am   Kids get on the bus, Mom and Dad get
ready for work

* * *

5:30 pm   Dinner time at the table as a family

6:00 pm   Clean the dishes, do chores, evening
baths

6:30 pm   Evening prayers, Scripture reading,
saints' lives

7:00 pm   Kids' bedtime

7:30 pm   Mom and Dad say prayers together

This schedule has worked well for our family of young children, but it doesn't happen every day. Some days we have company, others we are sick, sometimes the nibblets need to go to bed right after dinner and so prayers are very short. Whatever the reason for not doing something, you can almost always find a reason for doing it. Just because we skip one night does not ruin our week; nor does it preclude picking up the pieces the next night and starting all over again. —Caleb

We always find time for the things that are important to us. If we determine to make building our little church a priority, we will find the time necessary to accomplish our goal. Take small steps. Make mistakes. Find the rhythm that works for you. Your house is an extension of the parish and a microcosm of Christ's Church. Learn to celebrate this and make your home a place where prayer, silence, work, and sacred fellowship are the norm rather than the occasional treat.

When a good routine has been arranged, if both parents happily and firmly announce the plan, the children will ultimately accept it. There will likely be an initial success followed by the children testing the new boundaries, but when they find that their parents have firmly and joyfully held to the new structure, they will accept it as a part of their family's tradition. It's important for parents to remember that they have been crowned as king and queen of their home and that they—not their children—will be held accountable for the spiritual life of the family.

The Bjeletich family includes children ranging from preschool to high school, so the children's schedules do not line up nicely. Over the years, we've developed a routine that works for us.

Morning:

In the summer, when school is not an issue, the kids are all up by ten and gather together to say prayers at the icon corner.

During the school year, the children leave for school at different times, so family prayer is not possible. In our home, the elementary children leave by seven, the middle schoolers by eight, and the high schoolers and preschoolers by eight-thirty. Mom is up with the kids all morning, getting each of the groups underway in three waves; children are dressed, lunches are assembled, water bottles are filled. On a good, calm morning, we say short prayers together before we leave, and on more frantic mornings, we say prayers along the way in the car.

Evening:

Kids arrive home from school anywhere between two and five, and some will stay late for theater or basketball practice on any given day. Our family prioritizes eating together, so the timing of dinner is flexible to maximize the number of people present. Dinner can happen anywhere from five to seven-thirty and is always followed by the kids cleaning up.

Because our children's ages vary so much, their bedtimes range from eight to ten-thirty. Just before the youngest children go to bed (at or around eight), all other activities cease and everyone gathers together at the icon corner for evening prayers. Our large, active family requires a flexible routine, but because we all understand that evening prayers are critical and non-negotiable, we very rarely miss them. —Elissa

This is true in all areas of family commitment. If a family attends the Divine Liturgy only on the occasional Sunday, the kids (and parents) will struggle against it. Because the children know attendance is inconsistent and therefore negotiable, they negotiate. When attendance every Sunday is the standard and simply always happens, the Divine Liturgy is accepted as a natural and inevitable part of the routine, and the entire family falls into the rhythm of it. This is the case with all aspects of the home's rhythm: If mom and dad present a clear and permanent structure, it becomes a natural and necessary part of the family dynamic, like eating meals and brushing teeth.

This does not mean you will never encounter pushback from your kids on Sunday morning or that they'll willingly jump to prayer or sit like statues while you read the Scriptures. What you can count on is that your little humans will have good days and bad and will express varying opinions and feelings about your family's piety. When these rhythms and rules become a part of your family culture, you'll be raising children who understand the spiritual Christian life as a normal and necessary aspect of home life. As they grow, conversations about why and how we pray and worship will naturally emerge.

Times for Prayer

The most common time for family prayer is in the evening. It is a beautiful tradition to come together as a family to close the day in prayer. If we wish, however, to truly ground our family's rhythm in prayer, we should also begin our days glorifying God and thanking Him for a fresh new beginning.

If your family spends its mornings wildly hunting lost items and rushing out the door, give this a try: Gather your children before an icon and quietly say a beautiful morning prayer together before you head out. Taking a moment to remember God and the blessings He has heaped upon us will bring some peace to our hearts and set us on a good path for the day.

Some families will have an icon in the car and prop it up on the console to say morning prayers on the road. While this may not be as peaceful as standing before the icons at home, we will at least remember God as we begin our day.

In my car, I have a little compartment above the rear-view mirror for sunglasses. We've taped some small icon cards and a cross up there to create an iconostasis of sorts. On the mornings when prayer time falls prey to chaos, we pray in the car. And when we drive past an accident or hear sirens, down comes the iconostasis for a spontaneous group prayer for those affected. —Elissa

A particularly wonderful Orthodox tradition is to cross ourselves and bless our food and drinks before we consume them. In this way, we acknowledge that our bodies are indeed temples of God, refusing to bring anything that is not blessed into this holy body. More than simply expressing gratitude for our food, the Orthodox ask for God's blessing, that He might allow us to be nourished both physically and spiritually by each meal.

Begin now to make a habit of crossing yourself before eating or drinking, saying a quiet prayer. When you're just preparing a small snack, the prayer can be as simple as, "Lord, bless the food and drink of Your servants." At the table with your family, let it be a large and wonderful prayer with which Christ Himself is invited to join you.

Sample Daily Rhythm
Morning
Wake up & get dressed
Morning prayers at icon corner
Breakfast (opening with blessing of the food)

School hours
Lunchtime
Blessing of the food before eating
Evening
Homework and reading time
Dinner (opening with blessing of the food)
Bath time & pajamas
Teeth brushing
Evening prayers at icon corner
Story time—daily Gospel reading or Bible story or saint's life
Bedtime & tuck-ins

With a simple rhythm like this, the family is praying together at least five times a day. By blessing our meals and gathering at the icon corner twice daily, we introduce a rhythm that is firmly grounded in prayer.

In each family, these routines will take their own shape; some families prefer to pray immediately after dinner, while others wait until just before bed. Some parents will offer story time in the morning, while the children are fresh.

In larger families, bedtime is not always at the same time for each of the children. If your family begins to outgrow this common schedule, you can always make adjustments while keeping the rhythm and unity of the family. For instance, everyone can join together for prayers and the daily reading after dinner, and then children can head off for bed one at a time, as is age-appropriate. Family prayer is essential, and it should be prioritized—but the timing will vary for each family. It is best if families work out their own rhythm, so long as the critical elements of family prayer and study are always included.

WHAT ABOUT THOSE TIMES WHEN YOU JUST CAN'T DO IT?
Naturally, there is no need to be legalistic about these rhythms, and when extraordinary circumstances arise, the rhythm should be flexible. For instance, if the family is out late visiting friends or attending an event, you might do your evening prayers in the car so that you can quickly heap the little ones into bed when you arrive home. If a child is sick and cannot come to prayers, the family might go to his bedside to pray. If a morning is rushed, perhaps those prayers will be said in the car or at the breakfast table. The important thing is to make room for prayers in your routine.

> If you do not feel like praying, you have to force yourself. The Holy Fathers say that prayer with force is greater than prayer unforced. "The Kingdom of Heaven is taken by force." (Matthew 11:12) —St. Ambrose of Optina[21]

CHAPTER 6

Finding a Prayer Rule

Prayer rule? That sounds incredibly unpleasant. There is nothing I need less than more rules in my life!

Right off the bat we encounter a struggle in Orthodox vocabulary. For new converts, or for those cradle Orthodox rediscovering their faith, there can be a lot of confusion when it comes to the words we use for the practices or traditions (usually in another language, which also makes things confusing) which are central to the Orthodox spiritual life. "Rule" is one of those words. Perhaps it would be best to begin by addressing this vocabulary.

The religious life of our house has been in a constant state of flux from day one. How often should we pray? What should we pray? Where should we pray? We tried to do a lot of things the right way and got discouraged when our plans didn't work for longer than a few days. Because we had no clear direction or shared vision, we ended up burning out and not praying at all. Our family's piety was restricted to Sunday morning worship. It wasn't until my wife and I discovered Orthodoxy and started the process of conversion that all the "shoulds" quieted down and we started to see our family's piety in a different light. Rather than a hodge-podge of possibilities, the Church provided us with order, a system, and a set of guidelines to follow. It hasn't been all prosphora and prayer ropes since then, but the stress and frustration lifted when we reframed our quest for family holiness in light of the Church's teachings on personal piety. —Caleb

When you hear Orthodox writers and speakers mention the prayer rule, they're using a truncated form of the word ruler. It's a translation of the word we use to describe the canon of Scripture or the canons of a council. Canon comes from the Greek *kanon*, which means "guideline." (Originally it meant the clearly marked lines in a race course.) So a prayer rule, in its most simple definition, consists of those prayers we try to say each day when we say our prayers. For each Orthodox person, the guidelines will be a little different. The rule could be shorter or longer, include psalms, or even a daily reading of the Liturgical Hours. But this standard marks the path we keep to when saying our prayers.

The goal of prayer in the Orthodox life is the breath of the Spirit. St. Theophan the Recluse says, "If there is prayer, the soul lives; without prayer, there is no spiritual life."[22] In simple terms, the foundation of your little church is held together by your prayer life. If your family and personal prayer life are strong and robust, you will see success in other areas of spiritual development. If they aren't, then other areas will also struggle. On one hand, it's a simple matter of discipline in one area of life breeding success in others. Daily prayer isn't a good-luck charm, guaranteeing success in all endeavors. It is a necessary element; it is not a bag of magic beans.

Some Typical Prayers

From this point on, start incorporating a new word into your personal vocabulary: *typica*. It's a Greek word, but for us native English speakers, it's the root of the word *typical*. Rather than thinking in terms of a regulation (from the Latin meaning "little king"), start thinking in terms of the typical prayers that make up your day. Below are some typical prayers Orthodox have used, and continue to use, in daily practice. Most of them can be found in any Orthodox prayer book.

The Our Father ("The Lord's Prayer")
O Heavenly King, the Comforter
Holy God, Holy Mighty, Holy Immortal
Psalm 50/51
The Morning Prayer of Metropolitan Philaret ("Grant me to greet the coming day in peace...")
Rejoice, O Virgin
It is truly meet
Glory to the Father
The Jesus Prayer
The Prayer of the Hour

Psalm 22/23
The weekly Psalter schedule

And this is a short list! With the overabundance of prayers available, it's vital that we have some help and guidance along the way. Remember, start small. It's amazing what we can accomplish when we begin.

A good starting place for building any typical prayer rule might be the Trisagion Prayers. This phrase refers to a specific set of short prayers that are prayed in every Orthodox service, regardless of jurisdiction. They are like the first building block on which other prayers are stacked. (Note that there is also a service called the Trisagion for the Dead, which begins with these prayers but then continues with some memorial prayers for the departed. That is not what we mean here. The Trisagion Prayers begin with "O Heavenly King" and then continue to "Holy God, Holy Mighty, Holy Immortal," "O Most Holy Trinity," and the "Our Father.") There are various translations, of course, so you should use whichever translation you like. See the Resources section for some prayer books you might like to try.

Some families will begin with the Trisagion Prayers as the foundation of their prayer rule and allow it to grow from there. Regardless of what form your prayer rule takes, this is a good starting point.

Of course, if your children are very young or if the Trisagion feels overwhelming, starting out by praying just the Lord's Prayer (the last of the Trisagion prayers, beginning at "Our Father in heaven") may be a better fit for your family.

Before expecting your children to fall in line without hesitation, make sure personal prayer is a part of your daily discipline.

This doesn't mean you shouldn't start praying until you have perfectly mastered personal prayer—you may never begin! Let this be an encouragement, though, that it is vital to the success of your family's prayer rule that the parents are making the effort to pray daily, no matter how briefly. Keep this in mind as we move through this chapter. Parents are the workmen who are building the little church, and the children will take their religious cues from them.

Prayer Rule Example #1: Caleb's Family

As a family with four young children, our family prayer rule is very simple. We have tried many permutations of the prayer books available for print and online. We even tried praying the Compline each night, but we always return to the same basic family prayer rule, which works for us without fail and has begun to show the fruits of personal prayer for our older children.

The Shoemaker Family Prayer Rule

Little Girl 2: Glory to the Father...
Little Girl 1: Glory to Thee our God...
Everyone: O heavenly King... Holy God... Most Holy Trinity... and then we sing Our Father...
After the Trisagion prayers, we celebrate a small ceremony of forgiveness, in which everyone

prostrates before siblings, spouse, and children and asks forgiveness for the specific sins of the day. Everyone closes by singing It is truly meet…

When prayers are done, one parent reads a chapter or two from the Gospels and then whatever bedtime story we happen to be working on. —Caleb

Prayer Rule Example #2: Elissa's Family

When our first daughter was just a toddler, we developed a simple family prayer rule. First, everyone shared their "Thank You," such as "I am grateful for Mommy and Tata and for my grandparents and friends" or "I am thankful for our home and our food." Then we said the Lord's Prayer together and headed off to bed. When grandparents or friends visited, it was always a joy to hear them list what they were thankful for as well.

We decided later that we were ready to increase our prayer rule, and we began to say the Trisagion Prayers after our Thank Yous every night.

As our girls became stronger readers, we printed up a few small prayers we'd found in our prayer book, leaving them loose in a drawer. Each night, every girl chose a prayer from the drawer to read. This allowed them to customize the prayer rule

themselves, encouraging them to feel ownership of our family prayer experience.

Within a few years, we added simple intercessions (the reading of names from our list) and a closing prayer: Into Your hands, Lord Jesus Christ my God, we commend our souls and our bodies. Bless us, have mercy on us, and grant us everlasting life. Amen.

After prayers, our older kids generally head off after the closing prayer to finish up homework or watch TV. We encourage them to follow up with bedtime prayers, but each child works out their personal efforts privately. Our priest counsels them on their individual prayer rules, and Marko and I stay out of it. —Elissa

Prayer Rule Example #3: Jared's Family
We cross ourselves, and since my children have speech delays, we just do Lord Have Mercy and we have them pray for their friends and family. I try to say the Trisagion beforehand.—Jared, father of two young boys

These are the first steps. The goal is not to say every prayer in your book, but simply to make prayer part of your family's culture and daily routine. St. Paisios the Athonite offers instructions to parents that emphasize inviting children to participate.

"Mom and Dad will be praying, please join us."

"Please don't interrupt us."

"Please stand for the Our Father."

"Thank you for praying with us."

These make for a much warmer conversation than a litany of "shhh" and less-than-gentle suggestions to sit down and be quiet. Forcing children to pray leads to frustration. They will fight and resist, you will become angry, and you'll want to give up on this whole family prayer thing altogether. More importantly, you'll be standing together, angry and frustrated—but perhaps not actually praying. But a gentle guiding hand of loving parents welcoming children into family prayer time will show them prayer as a sweet, enjoyable time of fellowship and communion with God and with one another.

I think that the best thing, in my limited experi- ence, is to simply invite your child into your prayer life with you, and to trust God to reveal Himself to your child as you yourself pray. If the child sees you being devout, and that is an open space for the child to enter, the child will be instructed by the Holy Spirit. Obviously, individual kids will have individual needs—my son is nineteen months and knows that we are praying, and I'll try to give him an icon or prayer rope or candle to hold while I pray aloud. I encourage him to do his cross, which he started doing on his own after seeing others and

us do it. It's about inviting the child into the space
that prayer makes for us to be with God, and pay-
ing attention to God yourself. —Allison, mother of
one toddler

Intercessory Prayer

Intercessory prayers are the prayers we say for the people in our lives. There's even a prayer at the evening litany for "those who have asked us to pray for them, unworthy as we are," because the Church knows we forget to pray for people—even when we say we will. Making intercessions a regular part of your personal and family prayer rule is a powerful way to connect your family to those who are suffering, sick, alone, or departed.

Intercessions work well just before you begin, or just before you finish, your family prayers. Mom and Dad can sit down with their children and make a list of the people they want to pray for especially that day. With these names in our hearts and their needs in our minds, we can approach our daily prayers with special intention to pray for those particular people as well as ourselves.

Keeping track of your intercessions or specific prayer requests can be as simple as writing down each person's name on a piece of paper and keeping it in the family icon corner. There are also commemoration books available for purchase, but something as simple as a small notebook or a collection of 3 x 5 cards is just as effective. Remember, it's about taking small steps. Some families post the list in plain view in the prayer corner, while others keep it tucked away in a book. You can't do this wrong. Prayers for our loved ones, friends, and those who have departed keep our family in contact with Christ's Church around the world and through-out eternity.

> *When a friend is sick and misses a playdate, or*
> *when illness strikes someone we know, our children*
> *often add the names to the intercession list on their*
> *own. As soon as they can write, it's good to leave*
> *the list available to them, so that they can call the*
> *whole family to prayer on behalf of someone they*
> *love. —Elissa*

Reading the Prayers

Once children are old enough to read, it is a good idea to get them their own copies of the prayer books you're using. You could buy several copies, or you might consider printing up your family's customized prayer rule. You can find the translation you prefer online and lay out the prayers in the order your family prefers; then print enough copies for the whole family and any guests who may periodically join in.

> *A very special time of prayer in our family is when*
> *we get to pray together with the godparents of our*
> *children. The children love to show their icons to*
> *their godparents, and Mom and Dad get to share*
> *a special time with these dear friends together in*

prayer. This is always an extra special occasion and makes wonderful memories for each member of the family. —Caleb

Elder Paisios on Prayer in the Family

—Geronda, should the entire family pray the *Apodeipno* (Compline prayers) at night?

—The older family members should bestir themselves with nobility. They should lead by example. They should read the *Apodeipno* and say to the younger family members, "You can stay with us for a little while, if you want." If the children are somewhat older they can set up a rule; for example, fifteen minutes for the older children; two to five minutes for the younger children; and after that, as much as they want. If the parents make them stay for the entire *Apodeipno*, they'll just end up resenting it. They mustn't pressure them, because they haven't yet grasped the power and value of prayer. For example, parents can eat beans and meat: they can eat all types of foods. But when a little child is still only drinking milk, are his parents going to tell him to eat meat just because it's more nutritious? It may be nutritious, but the poor child can't digest it. This is why small children are given just a little meat and broth to start out with, so they'll want more.

—Geronda, sometimes adults are so tired in the evening that even they can't pray the *Apodeipno*.

—When they are very tired or sick, they should just pray half of the *Apodeipno* prayers, or at least say the Lord's Prayer. They shouldn't bypass prayer altogether. As in time of war, if at night you find yourself alone on a hill and surrounded by the enemy, you'll fire an occasional shot to scare the enemy away and keep him at bay. They, too, should let out a shot of prayer to keep the devil away.[23]

Really Praying

> *Teaching them to say prayers is easy, teaching them to pray is harder. Look out for life situations that lend themselves to teaching about different types of prayer—thanksgiving, supplication, asking forgiveness.* —David, father of seven

For many of us, prayer can be an intimidating task. It's easy to feel like a fool, standing in your icon corner offering prayers to an unseen God, hoping that He'll listen to you and help you in your troubles. After all, in movies and television, isn't it the fool who prays while the level-headed solve their own problems?

But for the Orthodox Christian, prayer is essential to our daily lives. When we understand that through prayer we encounter God and His saints and by their assistance grow in grace, the feelings of foolishness pass, and we begin to view ourselves in a new light.

> But I repeat: Remember, all of this is a guide. The heart of the matter is: Stand with reverence before God, with the mind in the heart, and strive toward Him with longing. —St. Theophan the Recluse[24]

We may need to pray for the gift of longing, actually asking God to make us yearn for Him; but once we have established that yearning in our hearts, we will no longer feel foolish as we pray.

We expect to have seasons—drier seasons when our prayers do not flow easily, and better seasons when prayer comes easily and naturally—but when we are faithful to our prayer rule, even the dry seasons yield spiritual fruit.

CHAPTER 7

Fasting as a Family

Today is the joyful forefeast of the time of abstinence,
the bright threshold of the Fast. Therefore, brethren,
together let us run the race with confident hope and
with great eagerness.
                    —Ode 1, First Canon of Cheesefare Monday

What Is Fasting?

According to the Church's teaching, fasting is a means to an end: salvation. Our Lord instructed His disciples that certain demons could not be overcome without fasting; the judgment of God was turned away from Nineveh because of fasting; the message of salvation was brought to the gentiles in part because Peter was fasting.

St. Matthew records in the Sermon on the Mount the way in which Christians are to approach fasting—with joy and gladness, not with self-pity and overt shows of piety:

"Moreover, when you fast, do not be like the hypocrites, with a sad countenance. For they disfigure their faces that they may appear to men to be fasting. Assuredly, I say to you, they have their reward. But you, when you fast, anoint your head and wash

your face, so that you do not appear to men to be fasting, but to
your Father who is in the secret place; and your Father who sees
in secret will reward you openly." (Matt 6:16–18)

Christ does not say "if you fast" but "when you fast," because fasting is as central to the Christian life as prayer. As the children of
Israel prepared to meet God at Sinai with fasting for three days, so
we prepare ourselves to receive Him. (This passage from Exodus
is read on Holy Thursday as we prepare to meet God on Pascha.)

Many Orthodox Christians struggle with fasting. Many converts see the rules as the Church's mandates for behavior and a
strict diet. Some who were raised in the Church never fasted as
children and have never been instructed in the proper mindset
nor in the Church's teachings about feast and fast.

Those outside the faith see fasting through a multifaceted lens
of other religious traditions or fad diets. One convert finds she
must explain to her mother each year that Great Lent is not like
Ramadan; and that no—she, a nursing mother, is not expected to
keep the fast with the same strictness as others, nor will she need
to "make it up" later. With so much misinformation and confusion, what are the builders of the little church to do as they seek
to incorporate this ascetic practice into their family?

The Church upon the "bright threshold of the Fast" looks for-
ward with eagerness, and yet we frequently speak of fasting as if
it were a dreaded burden. We are anxious about what we'll eat;
we wonder if we'll have the strength to complete the fast. Often,
because we are overly focused on the food, we fail to see that fasting is a beautiful and joyful opportunity and to treat it with the
eagerness it deserves.

One should not think about the doings of God when one's stomach is full; on a full stomach there can be no vision of the Divine mysteries. —St. Seraphim of Sarov[25]

The saints teach us that we can better perceive God's holy mysteries if we are fasting; somehow, when we are not satiated by rich foods and overindulgence, our hearts are more open and perceptive, and we begin to understand God in our lives. Think about how your body is better prepared to pay attention and focus when you are a little hungry compared to the lull in attention and energy after lunch, or after an indulgent Thanksgiving dinner. Fasting works on this principle: we are better prepared to meet God and see His works when our body and brains are honed by a little hunger. All you need to do is remember how you felt after Thanksgiving dinner last year—when all you wanted to do was lie down on the couch and (perhaps) sleepily watch the football games.

This doesn't mean that meat and dairy products are bad, or that the Church wishes for us to punish our bodies or to deprive ourselves. We human beings are easily distracted—easily caught up in the pleasures of the world—so we learn to take breaks. Because the Church recognizes that all blessings (including food) come from the hands of a loving Father who has called each one "good" (Genesis 1), we reject the idea that any food could be evil in itself. The Holy Church sets aside some time for fasting, for holding back from the pleasures of food and worldly entertainments, so that we can focus on God, and then balances fasting with periods of feasting. By striking this balance, we come to find more joy in the bounty He provides us.

Some do [fast] and others have diet restrictions as prescribed by the doctor. Fasting would be more successful if the parents model the practice and if they can creatively cook fasting food well. —Yola, *mother of three*

Of course, fasting is not magic. Like every aspect of Orthodox life, this is not a formula for a perfect experience—it is the framework for a struggle. Fasting is not supposed to be easy. It's tempting to imagine ourselves wonderfully fulfilling all the requirements of the fast and standing before an icon in quiet contemplation of the Lord; but it's more realistic to expect that we'll be grumpy and short-tempered, and that those very mood swings will prove to us how reliant we are on rich comfort foods and how important it is to shift that reliance to God.

Fasting produces humility. This is a great blessing, but know that means we can expect to be humbled by the struggle. It's going to be hard.

Control your appetites before they control you. —St. John Climacus

Fasting Is Not a Diet

A fast is not the same thing as a diet. Plenty of people will embark on juice fasts and cabbage soup diets. You'll find vegans in every walk of life. Many people will follow a diet, but they will not be fasting. They will exercise self-discipline and will free themselves from the passions associated with rich and fattening foods, but their diet will not soften their hearts or bring them closer to God.

> Bodily passions or passions concerned with material things are reduced and withered through bodily hardship, while the unseen passions of the soul are destroyed through humility, gentleness and love. —St. Theodoros the Great Ascetic[26]

Fasting from foods is only an effective spiritual tool when we combine it with prayer, almsgiving, and fasting from sin. When we practice humility, gentleness, and love, we are defeating the other passions that keep us from God. A true faster will not only abstain from food but will fill his or her days with almsgiving and charitable acts, with study of the Scriptures, and, most importantly, with an intensified effort at prayer.

> I have said these things, not that we may disparage fasting, but that we may honor fasting; for the honor of fasting consists not in abstinence from food, but in withdrawing from sinful practices; since he who limits his fasting only to an abstinence from meats, is one who especially disparages it. Dost thou fast? Give me proof of it by thy works! If thou seest a poor man, take pity on him! If thou seest an enemy, be reconciled to him! If thou seest a friend gaining honor, envy him not! —St. John Chrysostom[27]

Practically speaking, this makes the fast an even more difficult struggle. We must watch what comes out of our mouths even more carefully than what goes into them. In those very moments when we are short-tempered and irritable because we have not indulged in those comfort foods that keep us mellow, we are asked to resist yelling at our kids and snapping at our spouses. The fast is not only about eating but about making a sincere effort to love one another, to be kinder, gentler, and humbler.

How Fasting Works

Learning to fast begins with understanding which foods we're giving up and when. Ideally, all Orthodox Christians would fast with exactly the same rules, so that our offering could be the same; but in practice, there are regional, jurisdictional, and personal variations. That is to say that some bishops and priests allow their people small exceptions here and there, and this produces somewhat less consistency in the fasting. In addition, some cannot keep the full fast for medical reasons.

You can find the official fasting guidelines on a liturgical calendar, which can be purchased from your parish bookstore or online. There are also a number of apps available for download for phone or tablet. These calendars will tell you the daily lectionary (the Bible readings for the day), the saints that are celebrated that day, and exactly which foods are allowed on each day.

On the calendar, you will see strict fast days, sometimes marked with a small cross, on which we are called to avoid:

» meat, including poultry and any meat products such as lard and meat broth

» eggs and dairy products (milk, butter, cheese, etc.)

» fish (meaning fish with backbones; shellfish are always permitted)

» olive oil

» wine

On the calendar, you will also see wine and oil days, often marked with a small picture of grapes, when wine and oil are permitted.

Some fast days will be labeled "fish, wine, and oil days," perhaps marked with an image of a fish.

Fasting practices vary by region and jurisdiction. You may find that in your parish, fish is normal fare on strict fast days, considered roughly equal to shellfish. In some jurisdictions, the restriction on olive oil is not observed, while in others it is expanded to include all pressed oils and margarine. Some people interpret the restriction on wine to include all alcoholic beverages, while others interpret beer and cider to be allowable when wine is not.

> *We've tried the full fast several times, but I admit that we are bad at it. So we do our best at removing meat, but we usually have dairy even during Lent. We try to do the Wednesday/Friday fast throughout the year a bit more strictly. Partly it's because we are still in the blur stage that's so physically demanding of a mother. I hope to keep getting better at it. Fasting was not part of my upbringing, so I have had to learn how to cook differently.*
> —*Nicole, mother of three*

Speak with your priest to understand how your parish is fasting. In general, it is good (especially in our first years of fasting) to fast as the community fasts, so that we are supporting one another and experiencing a common fast. If your parish does not fast, you might consider finding a parish that does so that your efforts can be supported.

The focus should be on small meals of simple fare. This is not a time to gorge ourselves on Lenten food—did you know marshmallow fluff is vegan?—but a time to leave a little physical hunger, which will help us focus on our spiritual needs and develop a hunger in our soul for Christ.

Living the Church Calendar

We fast in community, which means the Church offers up one fast together. Unlike other Christian groups, where each individual chooses something to give up, in the Orthodox tradition (and truly, in all traditions predating the current modern period) we give up the same foods together, as one body. Compare this with the Church's other practices: common lectionary, common liturgy, common prayers. Even though there are slight differences between jurisdictions in the details, our Church offers up one sacrifice of praise and thanksgiving, says one creed, partakes of one communion. This focus on unity is enhanced in the way the Church approaches fasting seasons.

Think of the Divine Liturgy, in which the whole Church offers up one lamb (the prosphora) for Holy Communion. As the priest lifts up the bread and the wine, and we all lift up our hearts to the Lord, he calls out, "Thine own of Thine own we offer unto Thee, on behalf of all and for all!" The offering at the Divine Liturgy is given on behalf of all and for all; as one body we offer our hearts and the fruit of our labors—the bread and the wine—which will be transformed into the very Body and Blood of Jesus Christ.

The fast is not an individual offering, but an offering of the entire Church. Together, we make this joyful offering to our

good and loving God, and it is the wise Church's beautiful
liturgical calendar that provides the framework for fasting and
feasting in communion with one another.

The liturgical year is, in fact, expressed as a calendar, but
simply to identify it with a calendar would be totally inadequate.
[. . .] [I]n the liturgical year, we are called to relive the whole life
of Christ: from Christmas to Easter, from Easter to Pentecost,
we are exhorted to unite ourselves to Christ in his birth and his
growth, to Christ suffering, to Christ dying, to Christ in triumph
and to Christ inspiring his Church. The liturgical year forms
Christ in us, from his birth to the full stature of the perfect
man. According to a medieval Latin saying, the liturgical year is
Christ himself, *annus est Christus*.[28]

By living the liturgical year as a community, we join together to
receive Christ in His fullness over time.

The calendar includes four fasting seasons (Great Lent, the
Apostles Fast, the Dormition Fast, and the Nativity Fast), the
Wednesday and Friday fast days, and a few specific holy days on
which we fast (in particular, the date of the beheading of John
the Baptist, the Feast of the Elevation of the Cross, and the day
before Theophany).

In addition to these four fasting seasons and daily fasts, there
are four fast-free seasons when fasting is not permitted, and
Orthodox Christians are encouraged to feast with joy and gratitude. These fast-free seasons are:

» the period between the Nativity (Christmas) and Theophany (roughly twelve days)
» the week after the Sunday of the Publican and the Pharisee
» Bright Week (the week after Pascha) (In some jurisdictions,
   this period may extend to a full forty days.)

» Trinity Week (the week between Pentecost and the Sunday of All Saints)

These fasting and feasting seasons are in rhythmic harmony with one another: four fasts balanced by four feasts, specific days of abstinence and special days of feasting. The Holy Church prescribes a balance of fasting and feasting, and each becomes more meaningful and beautiful in light of the other.

We want to be careful to maintain that harmony in the little churches we are building in our homes, and it's important for all parents to remember that the Church is a hospital for sinners and not a courtroom. Parents should gently shepherd their families through the year with its times of fasting and feasting with joy and gladness, walking the road to salvation—with all its hazards—hand in hand with their children.

> *We only fast from meat. We eat dairy and eggs during fasts. During the year, we have a set menu on Wednesday (spaghetti) and Friday (Boca burgers and bean burritos). Our children eat what is placed before them when out with friends.* —Photini, mother of two

Many new fasters are inspired to begin with Great Lent. While this is an honorable and good beginning, many priests will advise us to begin with Wednesdays and Fridays. We are wise to work up to a longer-term fast from these shorter fasts, so if possible, begin the Wednesday and Friday fasting now. When the next fasting season arrives, you'll be better prepared to take on the longer fast.

> The holy fasters did not approach strict fasting suddenly, but little by little they became capable of being satisfied by the most meager food. Despite all this they did not know weakness, but were always hale and ready for action. Among them sickness was rare, and their life was extraordinarily lengthy. —St. Ignatius the God-bearer

Dietary Restrictions and Other Concerns

In many families, there may be medical conditions, food allergies, and intolerances which make fasting more complicated. If a particular diet is medically necessary and conflicts with the Church's fasting guidelines, the person's health trumps fasting; work with your priest to find a way to fast that does not interfere with your medical needs. Pregnant and nursing mothers are included in the list of persons who are medically unable to take on a full fast.

> If you cannot go without eating all day because of an ailment of the body, beloved one, no logical man will be able to criticize you for that. Besides, we have a Lord who is meek and loving (philanthropic) and who does not ask for anything beyond our power. [. . .] For there exist, there really exist, ways which are even more important than abstinence from food which can open the gates which lead to God with boldness. He, therefore, who eats and cannot fast, let him display richer almsgiving, let him pray more, let him have a more intense desire to hear divine words. In this, our somatic illness is not a hindrance. Let him become reconciled with his enemies, let him distance from his

soul every resentment. If he wants to accomplish these things, then he has done the true fast, which is what the Lord asks of us more than anything else. —St. John Chrysostom, "On Fasting"

There have been many great saints of the Church, including the modern St. Porphyrios, who could not fast for medical reasons. The Church does not require that we harm ourselves in the interest of the fast; if there is a true medical need, the person must be happily exempted from the fast. Naturally, those who cannot fast are encouraged to offer those other aspects of the fast—increased prayer, almsgiving, and study—so that they might benefit from the fast.

For most of us, however, this is not an all-or-nothing question. Our medical needs may require us to eat some meat or some dairy, but this does not usually mean that we cannot fast at all; perhaps we can fast from red meat and from some types of dairy products, but must allow a minimal amount of others to maintain our health. For instance, while a pregnant woman is forbidden to fast, she can certainly opt to eat chicken rather than steak and to drink a glass of milk rather than eat a piece of cheesecake. We should work these questions out with our doctors and priests and come to a plan that will encourage both physical and spiritual health.

It is very difficult for us to fast with the food allergies in the household. Three of the five people in the household have life-threatening allergies to different foods. The focus in our house is removing the junk food and a conscious effort to fast when possible not to endanger someone with the food selections. —*Jackey, mother of three*

We have many food limitations, and some in our household are in essence always keeping their diet in check. We do however, do less. We try to avoid unnecessary expenditures. We don't say that we will avoid pizza, necessarily, because we live in a busy household with three teenagers. We will however go for either the hot-and-ready type or a pop-in-the-oven one. We try to avoid snacking for those who can, and desserts. That being said, if we host a coffee hour during a fast period or bring food for a parish event, it is always within the fasting guidelines. We do not wish to discourage anyone else who is keeping the fast that is prescribed. —*Jared, father of three*

[Fasting] is still in major flux for us. My son is allergic to every major food allergen, and then a few more: gluten, dairy, soy, corn, nuts, fish, eggs, yeast, red meat. He also has sensory aversions, so the list of things he won't eat is three times that long. So, for years, we've begun fasts with a bit of a scoff . . . our whole life is a fast, for heaven's sake!

*But all the kids are getting older, and I find that
my own soul is not benefiting at all from this
perspective. So this year, we're trying the real deal,
all of us. I think we'll leave oil in the mix because,
with all his other difficulties, eliminating oil feels
pretty impossible right now. I hope to do a full fast
someday, but this is where we are now. —Maura,
mother of three*

Before embarking on a mad-dash effort to apply every one of the Church's teachings all at once, make sure you and your family are taking the advice and spiritual counsel of a wise priest or spiritual father. Be open and honest with him regarding your limitations, your concerns, your family's personal situation (for example, are you on public assistance with an overabundance of milk each month? are there health concerns?), and your plans for adapting the Church's fasting rules to your family life. Just as the fasting guidelines can be altered based on your health, the plans you devise at the beginning of a fast may also be subject to change. If the plan you've developed is not working, speak to your priest about adjusting it.

*If we fast we fast from TV and this is hard. We
don't have a lot of money and chicken is the most
reasonable thing to buy . . . plus right now because
I'm breastfeeding I'm not fasting so I don't have
[the children] fast either . . . the only place where*

we are fasting from food is on Sunday before com-
munion or before confession. Baby steps seem to
work best. I do try to fast with my tone of voice or
being quieter. Again, baby steps. —Nina, *mother*
of four

Leading Our Children

Our fast must be a love offering, an effort to soften and prepare the heart so that prayers are more powerful and God's presence is more palpable—so we have to find a way to lead our children to make a good and intentional fast. Forcing them to fast does not create a freewill offering, and yet as is true of most parenting, we must sometimes make our children do what is good for them. This includes eating a healthy meal or offering a well-deserved apology. They may not want to do it, but we must find a way to lovingly teach them to do it so that they learn.

Honestly, fasting is not something we have talked
much about in our family. My wife and I devel-
oped a rule when we first became Orthodox and
have worked to make fasting a regular part of our
family life, so that as our children grow they have
the habit already ingrained and can receive the
explanation for why we are eating a certain meal
(or not) when they ask for it. One step we have
taken is to have a set menu during Lent and the

Nativity Fast. We eat the same meals each week,
which helps to keep our menu simple, freeing up
our budget for giving and our minds from the
worry of what we'll cook for dinner each night.
This has been more difficult at some times than at
others—and we're still learning how to communi-
cate about fasting to our inquisitive older children.
The big thing to remember in all of this is that you
don't have to wing it. There are guidelines to help
you out, and your priest stands ready to help you
integrate fasting into your year. —Caleb

As parents, we must take the time to explain fasting to our children, but our example will be far more important than our words.
When we tell our children that a proper fast includes prayer,
study, and almsgiving, and then we practice a fast that involves
only hummus and soy, our children see it. If we say that the fast is
a joyful love offering, and then we fast in misery, overly focused
on the food we're serving, our children see it.

The best way to teach a child what a fast should be is to show
them. If we are happily eating less and feeding the hungry more,
if we are eagerly studying the Word of God and increasing our
prayers, our children will see our honorable fast—and its spiritual
rewards—and every word we have said to them will be proven
and made manifest.

Do you fast? Then feed the hungry, give drink to the thirsty, visit
the sick, do not forget the imprisoned, have pity on the tortured,

comfort those who grieve and who weep, be merciful, humble, kind, calm, patient, sympathetic, forgiving, reverent, truthful and pious, so that God might accept your fasting and might plentifully grant you the fruits of repentance. Fasting of the body is food for the soul. —St. John Chrysostom

It is difficult enough to learn to fast on our own, but for those of us who first attempt fasting after having created a family, we must lead even as we are learning. This can be a lot to handle and can become overwhelming. Pace yourself, and avail yourself of your priest's good advice.

When Do Kids Begin to Fast?

Those who are born into the Church often have a grandmother who makes the rules: she can tell you at what age the child should begin fasting, how old is too old to fast, and offer you clear restrictions and regulations for every day in between. She has come to those conclusions based on her grandmother's advice and on her own experience raising a family in the Church. Each grandmother varies. One says fasting rightly begins at eight, where another says it begins at fourteen. They're both equally confident in their declaration, but they disagree.

Because the Church leaves these types of details to the individual, individuals are able to experiment and find what works best in their particular family. Of course, when they present it to their grandchildren, they might act like it's a rule, but it's not. It's something that has been worked out on a case-by-case basis.

When converts come to the Church, we want to understand the system so we can follow it properly. That makes sense, but fasting doesn't quite work that way. Ultimately, this is the wisdom of the Church, allowing us to apply the spiritual medicine of fasting as needed to our growing, developing families.

> *During Wednesdays and Fridays and the longer periods of fasting we follow the fast fairly strictly. I make Lenten dinners at home, sometimes allowing cheese for some of the younger kids. They don't like it at first, but they get used to it. I try to bake with substitutes so we can have muffins, cookies, waffles, etc. I have made hot chocolate with almond milk on a cold day and they like that pretty well.*
> —Amity, mother of four

If your children are still very young, they have the opportunity to grow up in a home where fasting is simply a matter of course; this will make your job much easier. Even if they are already older, you can help to smooth the transition to fasting by offering fasting foods as part of your normal fare. If your children are comfortable with hummus and lentils, beans and vegetable soups, fasting days will not be a shock to their system.

Young children should not undertake the full fast but should be offered meat and milk or cheese at mealtime. They need not eat these at every meal, but parents should discuss with their doctors the specific dietary needs of children at different ages and respect those guidelines. It is important that children be well nourished during these important developmental years.

Many families will offer a Lenten family dinner each night,

serving only foods that are appropriate according to the liturgical calendar (naturally, taking care that a good portion of the food on the table is appealing to the children present). The younger children will be offered meats and dairy products at breakfast and lunch, but the whole family will enjoy a Lenten meal together every night. In this way, the nutritional needs of the children are covered, but the family also establishes the tradition of fasting together. Over the years, cooperatively, the parents will watch to see when each child is ready to take responsibility for his own fasting. This will surely vary by family and may even vary by child. If the parents can be patient and supportive and can lead by example, everyone will eventually get there.

We do fast. Our children have always fasted, so it is not weird for them. When they were younger, they were allowed to eat breakfast before Liturgy. As they approach puberty, we are expecting more from them such as not eating before Communion. We mostly eat at home and cook from scratch anyway, so they are not attached to fast food and junk food. So, giving up dairy and eggs during Lent is not too hard. Once again, it's just a normal routine they have grown up with. —Mother of two boys

What Comes out of Our Mouths

There is a common beloved maxim about fasting: What comes out of our mouths is more important than what goes into our mouths. This is very true; we aren't going to become holier by denying ourselves meat but screaming at our children. St. John Chrysostom famously warns,

> Let the mouth also fast from disgraceful speeches and railings. For what does it profit if we abstain from fish and fowl and yet bite and devour our brothers and sisters? The evil speaker eats the flesh of his brother and bites the body of his neighbor.[29]

What a powerful image—we might fast from fish and fowl, but we devour human beings!

We know that fasting is intended to be a struggle, so we should expect to be irritable and to feel frustrated during fasting seasons. The challenge is to be nice anyway. Those leading families must make a great effort to be kind and merciful to our kids, even when we are denied our favorite comfort foods. Be merciful at all times, and don't let irritability get the best of you. Be merciful to your children and to yourself. Fasting is hard. It's supposed to be hard.

> If thou, O man, dost not forgive everyone who has sinned against thee, then do not trouble thyself with fasting. If thou dost not forgive the debt of thy brother, with whom thou art angry for some reason, then thou dost fast in vain; God will not accept thee. Fasting will not help thee, until thou wilt become accomplished in love and in the hope of faith. Whoever fasts and becomes angry, and harbors enmity in his heart, such a one hates God and salvation is far from him. —St. Ephraim the Syrian[30]

Communion Fast

A communion fast is different from the regular fasting we have been describing. Generally speaking, no food or drink is taken before receiving Holy Communion; generally, this begins at midnight the night before a morning liturgy, or in the case of an evening liturgy, there may be a light morning and/or lunch meal, followed by a communion fast throughout the afternoon.

Opinions on when a child should begin to fast before Holy Communion vary, and as with all fasting, the schedule should be adjusted for the specific child and his or her needs. Many families begin by first asking the child to eat only a light fasting meal before church. Over time, you might talk with the child about undertaking a complete fast, and allow them to choose when they are ready to make this offering. Of course, if the child reaches some maturity (the teen years, certainly) and has not yet begun to attempt it, at some point the parent should require it.

Some eight- or nine-year-olds can skip breakfast with no problem, while other twelve- and thirteen-year-olds find themselves becoming light-headed and dizzy during the Divine Liturgy. Our goal is not to punish the body nor to cause a situation in which the child cannot be prayerful and attentive in church. Feel free to try a complete fast before communion and to pull back if your child seems to need to wait a little while longer before making that step. At all points, it is wonderful to speak with the child and the priest together about these decisions, allowing the child to properly take ownership of his or her own faith journey.

Marital Fast

Generally speaking, married couples are expected to fast from physical intimacy on fasting days (Wednesdays and Fridays, throughout the four fasts, etc.) Of course, there must be mutual consent, as St. Paul advises. At the very minimum, couples should fast before receiving Holy Communion and during Holy Week. As with all spiritual efforts, couples should consult their priest as they develop their marital fasting rule.

A Prayer for the Fast

When we say the prayer life intensifies during a fast, we are referring to the idea that we should attend more services during this time and make our prayer rule a little bit longer.

In the Orthodox Church, we have been given a special prayer that is very much beloved during fasting seasons, especially Great Lent and Holy Week. If it is not already in your prayer book, be sure to print this up and set it in your icon corner. Include this prayer in morning and evening prayers (as possible) throughout Great Lent and Holy Week. Soon, the whole family will have memorized and come to appreciate this beautiful prayer.

Lenten Prayer of St. Ephrem the Syrian

O Lord and Master of my life, give me not a spirit of sloth, idle curiosity, love of power, and useless chatter. Rather, accord to me, Your servant, a spirit of chastity, humility, patience, and love. Yes, Lord and King, grant that I may see my own faults and not condemn my brother, for blessed are You forever and ever. Amen.

For many years, this prayer was the extent of our fasting. My wife was pregnant, we had small children, and our finances were very tight, which ironically made fasting foods (fruit, vegetables, etc.) too expensive for our budget. It was this prayer that became the center of every fasting period. Our children have grown up loving this prayer, and it's still the highlight of each year—primarily because of all the prostrations ("big bows") we do as part of our family prayer rule. —Caleb

Fasting from Entertainments

In modern Western households, families—both Orthodox and non-Orthodox—struggle with managing time spent with digital entertainment sources, from television and movies and video games to smartphones and the myriad distractions they offer. While some of the products available are clearly vile, it is easy enough for parents to limit a child's choices to the more wholesome and less violent or morally reprehensible games, shows, and websites.

But even when the chosen entertainments are not dangerous or evil in and of themselves, they can be so attractive and mind-numbing that we find ourselves losing hour upon hour to them. People don't often think of this as a spiritual issue, but long before the invention of video gaming, in C. S. Lewis's *The Screwtape Letters,* Uncle Screwtape offers the following advice to his demon nephew about tempting his assigned human:

[A}s one of my own patients said on his arrival down here, 'I now see that I spent most of my life in doing neither what I ought nor what I liked.' The Christians describe the Enemy [God] as one 'without whom Nothing is strong'. And Nothing is very strong: strong enough to steal away a man's best years not in sweet sins but in a dreary flickering of the mind over it knows not what and knows not why, in the gratification of curiosities so feeble that the man is only half aware of them, in drumming of fingers and kicking of heels, in whistling tunes that he does not like, or in the long, dim labyrinth of reveries that have not even lust or ambition to give them a relish, but which, once chance associ- ation has started them, the creature is too weak and fuddled to shake off.

You will say that these are very small sins; and doubtless, like all young tempters, you are anxious to be able to report spectac- ular wickedness. But do remember, the only thing that matters is the extent to which you separate the man from the Enemy. It does not matter how small the sins are provided that their cumu- lative effect is to edge the man away from the Light and out into the Nothing. Murder is no better than cards if cards can do the trick. Indeed the safest road to Hell is the gradual one—the gentle slope, soft underfoot, without sudden turnings, without milestones, without signposts.[31]

The safest road to hell is to be gently lulled into thinking about anything except God. Entertainments need not be spectacu- larly wicked or even particularly interesting; if they keep us from prayer and from building a loving community in our homes, then they've succeeded in damaging our spiritual lives. The Psalm- ist writes, "Be still, and know that I *am* God" (Psalm 45[46]:11); but where will we find stillness when we keep busy with mind- numbing distractions? There is no peace for us when our minds are "drearily flickering" with these little distractions that neither feed us nor enrich our lives.

Traditionally, Orthodox fasting meant that dances and parties would be put on hold; many entertainments have always been reserved for feast seasons and proscribed during fast seasons. Entertainment in our modern culture now includes television and electronic devices, so we must add these to the list of behaviors to consider when working out our family's fast.

As with all fasting, we must prayerfully weigh what is appropriate and needful for our particular family. Different families will structure it differently. In a household where dietary restrictions make the food fast particularly hard to observe, the family may keep a total fast from entertainments to make up the difference. On the other hand, some children with special needs may relieve pressure from overwhelmingly difficult interactions by means of a technology break, and so their parents do not restrict gaming.

As parents consider whether to restrict or limit such entertainments during fasting periods, we should pray about it, we should speak to our priests, and we should spend a little time honestly charting how much of our family time involves parents or children sitting side by side but focused on devices and entertainments rather than on one another. The fast gives us the opportunity to curb all our passions and habits, offering seasons for pruning so they don't grow out of control. Limiting the types of entertainments and the amount of time spent on them during a fast period can be the antidote to one of our modern culture's insidious new problems and can help us clear out a serious obstacle to spiritual growth.

The Orthodox Rhythm: Fall Down, Get Up, Fall Down, Get Up. (Repeat.)

As we plan for an upcoming fasting season, collecting recipes and stocking our pantry, our confidence grows, and we begin to envision a really successful, impressive fast. Invariably, by the end of the fasting season, something has gone wrong: we've succumbed to temptation and eaten a cheeseburger, we've yelled at our children, we've gossiped about our neighbors. This isn't the end. This doesn't mean it's time to pack it in and hope for a better fast next time.

> My brethren, do all that is in your power not to fall, for the strong athlete should not fall, but, if you do fall, get up again at once, and continue the contest. Even if you fall a thousand times, because of the withdrawal of God's grace, rise up again at each time, and keep on doing so until the day of your death. For it is written: 'If a righteous man falls seven times,' that is, repeatedly throughout his life, 'seven times shall he rise again' [Proverbs 24:16]. —St. John of Karpathos[32]

When (we do not say if) we fall, we do not give up, but instead we get up again. We fall, we get up. Over and over again. There may be nights when, out of exhaustion, we feed our families an easy but completely non-fasting meal. Say a prayer, thank God for this food, and ask Him to help you do better. Don't give up; just get back up and keep working at it.

One afternoon late in Great Lent, my fifteen-year-old came into my room, exasperated. She said,

"Every year, I promise myself that this is the year
when I'm going to pull off a perfect Lent, and
every year I manage to screw it up! Mom, I was
almost there and then I completely forgot and ate
chicken at lunch today!" I couldn't help but laugh
and tell her, "Lent is supposed to humble us, so
I'm not at all surprised that God doesn't let you
puff up your ego with a Perfect Score for Great
Lent. That would be the worst Lent ever, actually,
because it would make you more arrogant instead
of humbling you." —Elissa

Fasting is intended to humble us. If we are truly humble, then we should not be surprised when we fall—but we should pick ourselves up, ask God to strengthen the first among sinners, and keep trying. When (not if) you fall, do not waste any time beating yourself up about it, but simply do your metanoia (bow or prostration) and begin again. This is how we practice repentance and humility.

> It is always possible to make a new start by means of repentance. "You fell," it is written, "now arise" (cf. Prov. 24:16). And if you fall again, then rise again, without despairing at all of your salvation, no matter what happens. So long as you do not surrender yourself willingly to the enemy, your patient endurance, combined with self-reproach, will suffice for your salvation. "For at one time we ourselves went astray in our folly and disobedience," says St. Paul, ". . . Yet He saved us, not because of any good things we had done, but in His mercy." (Tit. 3:3, 5) —St. Peter of Damaskos[33]

CHAPTER 8

Raising Good Stewards

It is the poor man who holds out his hand, but it is God Himself who receives whatever you give to the poor.

—St. John Chrysostom

In her wisdom, the Church has provided her people with the three foundation stones—the three tools—we have been discussing throughout the first part of this book. Her teachings show us that prayer, fasting, and almsgiving are the first tools in our workshop to combat the wiles of the enemy. Sometimes we disregard one or more of these disciplines because it seems more difficult or more complicated than the others. Fasting has a complex set of restrictions that vary between parishes and jurisdictions; prayer involves organizing our time around a rule. Almsgiving? Have you seen my checkbook? How can I afford to give any more money when we can barely make the budget balance?

It's difficult to be a parent. Our modern culture seems to have cornered the market on difficult spiritual climates—greed and materialism are pervasive, and our children aren't even safe when they go to school. The lure of possessions is especially prevalent in contemporary media. It's unavoidable. Everywhere we turn, we see proclamations that our lives would be in a sorry state indeed without expensive clothes, gadgets, and skin care products. No matter where we go to escape the siren song of stuff, we are met with greater and greater temptation to embrace discontent; we don't gratefully embrace the blessings we have, but instead we yearn for more, more, more.

> The Devil endeavours by every means to keep men in error, in the enticement of the passions, in darkness of mind and heart; in pride, avarice, covetousness, envy, hatred, wicked impatience and irritation; in evil despondence, in the abominations of fornication, adultery, theft, false-witness, blasphemy, negligence, slothfulness, and sluggishness. —St. John of Kronstadt[34]

Greed and insatiable lust were the temptations foisted upon Adam and Eve: Eat this, and you will be like God. Greed prompted Judas to betray Christ to the authorities:

> Judas loves money with his mind.
> The impious one moves against the Master.
> He wills and plans the betrayal.
> Receiving darkness, he falls from the light.
> He agrees to the price and sells the priceless one.
> As payment for the deeds the wretch gains hanging and a terrible
>   death.
> From his lot deliver us, O Christ God, granting remission of sins
>   to those who celebrate Thine immaculate passion with love.
> —Kathisma Hymn of Bridegroom Matins of Holy Tuesday

With greed apparently hardwired into our psyche, how can the little church hope to stand against the rising tide? How will the foundation hold when the rains come down and the floods come up? How do we as parents build on the stone foundations which are the commands of God when there are so many empty promises counterfeiting and offering false assurances? Just a quick glance over the Fathers and Holy Scripture will make it clear to even a casual reader that the way we use our resources is essential to a healthy spiritual life.

The truth is that being a parent is difficult in every time. In the Old Testament we read the story of Tobit and his wife Sarah—two Israelite captives of the Assyrian exile. They were bombarded with the temptations of power, greed, and selfishness even in their homeland. Their government had rebelled against Jerusalem and the Davidic kings, their forebears had set up and worshipped golden calves, and they were consistently ruled by more and more evil men who rejected the God of Abraham. Tobit, it seems, was one of a very few who remained faithful despite the expense and inconvenience. When the Northern Kingdom of Israel was conquered and exiled by the Ninevites, Tobit and his family lived under constant persecution from their king and their pagan neighbors.

One day, out of the blue, Tobit was struck blind and was left believing God had abandoned him. He and his wife quarreled, and he sat down—like Job—in the ashes to wait for death to take him. In his grief, he called to his son Tobias and advised him on how to live a holy life. Chief among his instructions are the three foundation stones of the little church: prayer, fasting, and almsgiving. Regarding almsgiving, Tobit advises his son:

> "Do almsgiving from your possessions to all who do righteousness. When you do almsgiving, do not let your eye be envious.

Do not turn your face away from any poor man, so the face of God will not be turned away from you. Do almsgiving based on the quantity of your possessions. If you possess only a few, do not be afraid to give according to the little you have. You are storing up good treasure for yourself in the day of necessity. For almsgiving delivers us from death and prevents us from entering into the darkness. Indeed, almsgiving is a good gift for all who do it before the Most High." (Tobit 4:7–11)

Compare Tobit's advice with Jesus' words from the Gospel:

"Take heed that you do not do your charitable deeds before men, to be seen by them. Otherwise you have no reward from your Father in heaven. Therefore, when you do a charitable deed, do not sound a trumpet before you as the hypocrites do in the synagogues and in the streets, that they may have glory from men. Assuredly, I say to you, they have their reward. But when you do a charitable deed, do not let your left hand know what your right hand is doing, that your charitable deed may be in secret; and your Father who sees in secret will Himself reward you openly." (Matt. 6:1–4)

When we take these examples from Scripture, together with the sayings of the Church about possessions and giving, we see a clear pattern emerging that addresses not only how to view our own possessions—as blessings from God—but also the remedy to the prevailing cultural wisdom that he who dies with the most toys wins. Below are some steps to take to help infuse the virtue of charity and almsgiving in your family and instill a right view of possessions into your little church.

Step One: Focus on the Giver

The earth is the Lord's, and its fullness,
The world and all who dwell therein. (Psalm 23[24]:1)

The Scriptures are replete with examples of the faithful turning to God as the source and provider of all good things. David's prayer at the end of his life and Job's response to the trials of Satan are just a few examples of Old Testament prophets understanding God as the source of all their material possessions. Throughout Sacred Tradition, the faithful have always turned from themselves to God when they struggle with the temptation to greed and avarice. The first step toward building a strong little church is placing Christ as the cornerstone.

"But who am I, and who are my people, that we are able to be zealous in offering to You? For all things are Yours, and of Your own we give to You. For we are strangers before You and sojourners, as were all our fathers. Our days upon the earth are as a shadow, and there are none that remain. O Lord our God, as for all this abundance which I have prepared that a house should be built to Your Holy Name, it is of Your hand, and all is Yours." (1 Chr. 29:14–16)

Then Job arose, tore his robe, and shaved off the hair of his head; and he fell to the ground and worshiped, saying, "Naked I came from my mother's womb, and naked shall I return. The Lord gave, and the Lord has taken away. As it seemed good to the Lord, so also it came to pass. Blessed be the name of the Lord." In all these things that happened, Job did not sin against the Lord or charge God with folly. (Job 1:20–22)

Before any family begins its walk toward freedom from possessions and control of its goods and money, it's important to take time to focus on the source of every good blessing. St. James reminds us that "every perfect gift is from above, and comes down from the Father of Lights" (James 1:17). Our journey must begin with the recognition that every blessing, every material and physical good, every spiritual blessing is a gift from God for the benefit of the individual, the family, the community, the Church, and the world. This is the first step toward freedom.

> Be earnest in righteous works, by which sins may be purged.
> Frequently apply yourself to almsgiving, by which souls are freed
> from death. —St. Cyprian

Here are some practical steps for families to begin to reorient their focus from material possessions to the Giver of those blessings:

» As a family, sit together and make a list of every good thing in your life. Thank God for each individual thing during family prayers.

» Develop the habit of thanking God for three specific things at the end of each day.

» Set aside a portion of your income to give to the work of the Church.

It's important for even young children to understand that the ultimate source of their blessings is their loving Heavenly Father. Christ Himself is called the Philanthropos—the lover of mankind—from which we derive the word *philanthropy*. When we give, we display most clearly the love of Christ. Parents might demonstrate this by sitting with their children and reading Philippians 2, noting how the Apostle Paul describes the philanthropy of Christ and holds it as an example to Christians.

"Have the same mind as Our Lord," the Apostle says, "who, though He was God, emptied himself and became a servant." It's a beautiful picture for our children and our families to contemplate and reflect on as we explore how we spend our time and treasure for the good of others. Read Jesus' words in the Sermon on the Mount in Matthew 5—7 and write down the number of times Jesus instructs His followers not to worry and to seek their provision from their loving Father.

Step Two: Reassign Value

Much of what prevents a family from becoming good stewards of the blessings God has given is confusion of values. Our society tells us the happiest man is young, single, wealthy, and attractive. The happiest woman is nineteen, well-coiffed, and technologically savvy. The happiest children are well-dressed, overfed, and have all the newest toys. Our definition of happiness is based almost exclusively on the things we have, the money we can spend, and the freedom from responsibility we see in young people. As a result, our values are stunted and our priorities are misplaced.

We cannot be free of our possessions so long as they continue to hold preeminence in our minds. As St. Thalassios said, "It is not difficult to get rid of material things if you so desire; but only with great effort will you be able to get rid of thoughts about them." If being good stewards were simply a matter of reducing our possessions or giving more money to a favorite cause, then the action would be simple and wouldn't require a chapter in a book. The reason we focus our attention on giving and living in submission to God's provision is that our possessions don't just belong to us; we belong to them and to the thought of them, to the desire to have and to hold onto them with all our strength.

Parents are the prime example of how to handle possessions for children. As in all things, children will learn from their parents before any external stimulus. If Mom and Dad are worried about money, fighting about bills, and struggling to keep up with the "happy" families we see on television, then children will learn this pattern for handling possessions. If, on the other hand, Mom and Dad hold their possessions lightly, give thanks for them, and give freely of their time and resources to those who have need, then children will see and respond to this behavior along with the heart attitude that births it. Before families can give with joy, they must see their value as people as greater than the value of their things and their bank accounts.

> *We talk about helping and giving. We encourage them to be the ones to place envelopes in the church box or talk about passing on items to other children. They're still very young, but we figure talking about it openly with them will set a good foundation for when they (and I) start venturing out of the house with more frequency.* —The deMorrow family

This is not a step that's easily broken down into manageable chunks. This is a matter of the heart and its alignment with Christ and His Church. St. John Climacus begins his Ladder of Divine Ascent with rejection of the world and submission to Christ. This rejection and submission will necessarily include the rejection of materialism and the vanity of possessions. It will be a continual struggle against our own will and the commands of Christ.

It's important for parents especially to go through this process of reassigning value with a trusted spiritual director and father confessor. Don't try to do this alone. Walking hand in hand, parents should begin this process of submission to the commandments together with their priest and confessor.

> *[Our children] go with us [on service projects] and are expected to help. They grow into this and start wanting to participate on their own. —Jackey, mother of three*

Step Three: Giving of Yourself

This chapter asserts several things about the topic of money and materialism in relation to the building block of almsgiving.

1. God is the giver of all good gifts.
2. The value we assign to items is extrinsic.
3. Giving and a compassionate lifestyle are signs of a healthy psychology.[35] The very act of giving promotes emotional and physical well-being, the effects of which compound and spread throughout the community.

If these assertions are true, then there is strong evidence to support the Church's teachings regarding almsgiving.

Here we need to diverge from the rhetoric of amounts and financial obligations—dues or tithes—and focus on the heart of giving, which promotes a healthier self, home, and society. This discipline of almsgiving, when separated from the other foundation stones of prayer and fasting, is simply a monetary benchmark for judging others or for self-promotion. When joined together, these three stones uphold the little church and support a healthy and pious life that celebrates and rejoices in the goodness of God. The question to ask of yourself and your family is not how much you can afford, but in what ways you can give to God's work of your time, treasure, and talents.

> *My daughter is interested in the animal welfare league in town, so we will probably make cat toys for the shelter during homeschool a few times. Autism Awareness Day is right before Pascha this year, too, so we might do something for that since our son has it and Autism Speaks is very close to our hearts. —Maura, mother of three*

St. Joseph the Hesychast said, "Send your treasures to the heavenly storage room. Deposit your wealth in God's Bank, distributing it to the poor, the orphan, the widows, so that you can receive a million times more in the Second Coming of Christ." It is this mindset we as parents want to instill in our children. Not only are our material blessings sent from our loving Father, but He can take all our gifts—however small or great—and multiply them in

His Kingdom. In a day when many see the Church as an opulent money-hoarder, we need to place our families at the forefront of those who see Christ on the street and turn to lift Him up by sharing our material blessings. The *Philokalia* puts it this way:

> A man is not saved by having once shown mercy to someone, although, if he scorns someone but once, he merits eternal fire. For 'hungered' and 'thirsty' is said not of one occasion, not of one day, but of the whole life. In the same way 'ye gave me meat', 'ye gave me drink', 'ye clothed me', and so on, does not indicate one incident, but a constant attitude to everyone. Our Lord Jesus Christ said that He Himself accepts such mercy from His slaves (in the person of the needy).

> If a man has one day provided for all of the bodily needs of the poor, but, being able to do so on the next day, neglects some of his brethren and leaves them to die of hunger, thirst, and cold—then he has neglected and left to die Him Who said: 'Inasmuch as ye have done it unto the least of these my brethren, ye have done it unto me.' (Matt. 25:40)

The material wealth we gather on earth is transitory and temporary and will not satisfy our hearts; but the treasures we lay up in heaven will never lose their luster. Our hearts are either here on earth, struggling for material wealth, or they're in heaven; there is no compromise. "You cannot serve God and mammon" (Matt. 6:24). You must either serve God or choose to serve material wealth instead. Every one of us must choose.

As you and your family go over the blessings God has given you and begin the process of reassigning value to your material possessions, it is a time to ask how you can give of yourself to serve others. Below are some suggestions for giving of yourself that don't limit our understanding of almsgiving to financial sacrifice—though that is certainly a worthy and holy action:

» Donate excess clothing to a local shelter.

» Serve regularly at a soup kitchen or food pantry.

» Place charitable giving at the top of your monthly budget—placing the priority spending on God's work.

» Make a donation to the beautification of your parish.

» Invite your priest's family to your home for dinner.

» Visit your parish shut-ins and send cards to those in nursing homes or the hospital.

» Teach Sunday school.

» Be a part of the parish council.

» Organize youth events in the parish.

» Collect diapers and formula to be distributed to new parents in the parish.

» Form a funeral guild to assist those who are bereaved by coordinating meals and transportation.

As you can see from the list above, there's no limit to the love you can show to your parish and community when you start to reassign value and prioritize your time and finances. Nothing on this list is overly taxing, and each one of them is a common-sense, practical solution to the question of almsgiving within a family.

As parents sit down together to explore how their family can be a healthy, vibrant little church, it's important not to overlook the question of almsgiving. Every family, regardless of income or social status, can help to build and strengthen the Kingdom of God in their home, parish, and community.

Note that our list includes many acts of charity in which we

offer our time and our talents even more than our financial treasure. It is worth noting Fr. Roman Braga's observations on the
American attitude regarding charitable giving:

> There is a mentality [in the U.S.] that writing your monthly
> check to a charitable society can put your conscience to rest,
> especially when at the end of the year you can claim your con-
> tributions as deductions. There is something lost when you have
> no personal, and thus spiritual, connection with the people you
> help. Here you never even know the people you help, because
> your gift is given in the abstract. If you write your check for
> charity you can sleep well, even if in the hospital a person dies or
> your neighbor is in need. Maybe they do not need your money,
> but they do need your smile, your comfort. —Archimandrite
> Roman Braga

Mother Teresa puts it more simply: "It's not how much we give
but how much love we put into giving." When almsgiving is an
act of love, it is easy to see why it occupies such an important
position in the foundation of a Christian home.

Concluding Thoughts

In building your little church, it's important to begin with a solid
foundation. For the Orthodox family, this foundation is threefold:
prayer, fasting, almsgiving. On this foundation the little church is
able to grow and to thrive as part of the larger Body of Christ and
local parish family.

Many families become bogged down in some of the building
blocks while ignoring a strong base for their piety. It's wonderful
to celebrate name days, Slavas, major and minor feasts, or to cook

special dishes passed down through generations. Each of these things is a blessing, but none of these in itself is the core of our struggle for salvation. Before we ran our marathon, we learned to walk; before we ate our first T-bone, we suckled our mother's milk. The same is true for your little church.

Tobit's instructions to Tobias are as applicable in the modern world as they were when the Scriptures were written. As parents we are presented with a sacred duty in bringing our spouse and our children to salvation. We can't do that apart from the life of the parish and the Church at large. It's also impossible to fulfill this task by ignoring our little church or by building without a foundation.

The act of almsgiving is as important as how you fast or how long you say your prayers. These three are interconnected in a mystical way that vivifies the rest of the building project. Begin today: Give of your time to your family by eating a meal together, saying your prayers, or attending a church service. Continue to serve and give of your time, treasure, and talents by singing in your parish choir, visiting the sick and elderly, or donating to a local animal shelter. The only limit to almsgiving is your imagination. The important part is realizing that we are giving back to God out of our love what He has so graciously given to us out of His own love for us.

> I do not believe one can settle how much we ought to give. I am afraid the only safe rule is to give more than we can spare. In other words, if our expenditure on comforts, luxuries, amusements, etc., is up to the standard common among those with the same income as our own, we are probably giving away too little. If our charities do not at all pinch or hamper us, I should say

they are too small. There ought to be things we should like to do and cannot do because our charitable expenditure excludes them. —C. S. Lewis[36]

CHAPTER 9

Growing Up

*Our teenagers have to reach on their own the stage of
adult conviction about the faith. This does not mean
'in isolation,' but 'from their own experience.' They
have to emerge as Orthodox adults because they believe
that Orthodoxy is true—that it shows us how God is
and how we are. Only such a faith will be enough to
preserve them in Orthodoxy throughout their life. Some
children grow naturally from childhood faith to adult
faith, without trauma. But we must not be astonished
that for many, this growth involves a deep questioning
and reappraisal of their childhood faith. We notice how
many very committed adults have reached their trust
in Orthodoxy after a certain period of lapse, sometimes
even going away from the Church.*[37]

From the day our children are baptized, they are full members
of the Orthodox Church. They are neither junior members
nor extensions of their parents, but full Orthodox Christians with
the same free will and potential as adult members. It is common
to hear children referred to as "the future" of the parish. This is
a lovely thought, but the nomenclature is all wrong. If we really

believe the words of the prayers said at baptism and chrismation, then we cannot simply categorize children into "the future." They are the parish *now*, fully invested in what happens around them.

If we are raising them in a consciously Orthodox home, in the little church and also in the larger Church, our kids will grow up understanding themselves as having an Orthodox identity. From their youngest years, they will know they are Orthodox. This may seem like a stretch, but this early identification with the "Tribe," if you will, is integral to retaining not only bodies in our congregations but faithful hearts in the Kingdom.

Don't underestimate this truth. My four-year-old and my six-year-old identify themselves to their friends as Orthodox and are quick to engage adults in theological conversation. It's sometimes humorous to hear first graders discussing their understanding of the Church, but it's interesting whenever my eldest says very matter-of-factly, "We're Orthodox. We're different." I don't know that she really understands what that means, but it's a part of her self-identity as a Christian—even among her friends. Your children are watching you, and they are looking to you for cues about what the Faith means in your home. Start to create this identity for them, set the bar high, and watch them rise. —Caleb

As they grow and develop on the long path from infancy to adulthood, some of our children may begin to question whether Orthodoxy is right for them or even whether God truly exists. This is not a cause for alarm but a natural part of human development. Indeed, in the Gospel of St. Mark, a man asked Jesus to cast out the spirits that were trying to destroy his child. "Jesus said to him, 'If you can believe, all things *are* possible to him who believes.' Immediately the father of the child cried out and said with tears, 'Lord, I believe; help my unbelief!'" (Mark 9:23–24). Most of our doubt is like this father's: we do believe, we have a seed of belief, and yet also some nagging part of us does not yet believe.

We plant the seeds of faith in our children, and in time God will help those seeds grow and blossom into true faith. Remember Jesus' parable of the Sower: some seed will produce a crop, and some will not. Our job as parents is to help make the soil healthy and ready to receive the words of the Gospel; God will bring the harvest.

We should not fear this process of testing faith and inviting growth, but instead we should help guide it. We can teach our children who struggle with doubt to pray the prayer of the father in the Gospel: "Lord, I believe; help my unbelief!" We can urge them to take their doubts to God, to reach out to Him as they struggle.

So a parent, apart from being ready to discuss the faith freely, may have to live through an anxious period of praying, waiting, standing back and letting go. We cannot assume that saintly mothers of saints in the Church calendar were always at ease about their children—what we can judge is how effective a parent's prayer can be. [. . .] We can teach our children to pray openly and honestly in time of doubt or questioning: 'Lord, show me the truth.' Such a prayer is more effective than Christian apologetics.[38]

The most important thing we parents can do is pray. We can ask that God heal our children and fill them up with profound faith. We can call in the saints and beg help from the guardian angels who watch over them. We can talk to their godparents and get counsel from their confessor. We have armies of help within our reach, and we must call for them urgently at all times throughout our children's lives.

> Pray and then speak. That's what to do with your children. If you are constantly lecturing them, you'll become tiresome and when they grow up they'll feel a kind of oppression. Prefer prayer and speak to them through prayer. Speak to God and God will speak to their hearts. That is, you shouldn't give guidance to your children with a voice that they hear with their ears. You may do this too, but above all you should speak to God about your children. Say, 'Lord Jesus Christ, give Your light to my children. I entrust them to You. You gave them to me, but I am weak and unable to guide them, so, please, illuminate them.' And God will speak to them and they will say to themselves, 'Oh dear, I shouldn't have upset Mummy by doing that!' And with the grace of God this will come from their heart. —St. Porphyrios[39]

We can advise and we can pray, but we cannot force a child to love God. God's gift of free will extends even to our children, because He wants their voluntary love as much as He wants ours. Our obedience to His will is a gift freely given, a true love offering. Free will is precious and inviolable, and our goal as parents is not to take away the free will of our children, but instead to raise them up in such a way that they are likely to freely choose to follow God and to be a part of the Body of Christ. Remember that of the Barna findings we mentioned in the Introduction, four of the five things that help to keep a young person in the Church are within the power of the parent to provide; but you cannot experience a personal encounter with God for your child. Our job is to point the way, to bring lovingly, to coax kindly, and to make the space available for the encounter.

> You parents should pray silently to Christ with upraised arms
> and embrace your children mystically. When they misbehave
> you will take some disciplinary measures, but you will not coerce
> them. Above all you need to pray. —St. Porphyrios[40]

Parents are crowned as king and queen, priest and presbytera, of their family and are given special honor by God, who calls their children to offer the same honor to their parents. After years of having easy credibility with our children, it can be very painful when the children grow into adolescents and stop trusting the information we give. We must not take it personally—these are growing pains of a natural developmental process in which they individuate and separate. It begins a time of growing mutual respect between parent and growing child, who is becoming a peer. In this process, we should expect to be humbled. God is faithful. He loves our children more deeply than we ever could, and He is always calling us back to His love and into His Church.

If your child is struggling, talk to your priest and recommend that your child also speak with him. Ideally, your priest knows you and your children and can help. In some cases, it makes sense simply to demand that everyone attend church together and that everyone behave respectfully in church.

> *During difficult adolescent periods, I have told my older children whether they are actively praying or not, they are expected to join the family at prayer time and for Sunday morning liturgies. They are expected to attend, to be respectful and quiet, but whether they are actively praying or not is their choice.* —Elissa

> *Once my siblings and I were of age, the only requirement from our parents was that if we lived with our parents, we needed to attend church. It didn't matter which one, or whether the services were mornings, evenings, or weekdays—so long as we were attending regular worship services. For a few months between a failed job and beginning my seminary degree, I lived with my parents. Coincidentally, this was when I started to explore liturgical theology. I attended a local Episcopal church while my parents attended the nearby Presbyterian church. This arrangement worked out well and showed mutual respect between parent and adult*

child (I was at that point twenty-three). It's not
unreasonable to require children living in your
house to attend services, and it's also reasonable to
allow them to explore other expressions of Christi-
anity—fully confident that your powerful prayers
will keep them close to the Church. —Caleb

While we may demand certain respectful behaviors, it's important that we don't attempt to control our children's faith. God
has given each of us free will for good reason: He wants our love
offerings, not forced prayers.

St. Porphyrios said, "It is not sufficient for the parents to be
devout. They mustn't oppress the children to make them good
by force. We may repel our children from Christ when we pursue
the things of our religion with egotism."[41] We must work to keep
our ego out of this process, and to offer our children an Orthodox
way of life without forcing and oppressing them.

It has been suggested that a person's understanding of what
God the Father is like is based on what his own father was like:
If his father was loving, he is more likely to feel the love of the
Father, but if his own father was abusive and angry, he is more
likely to think of God as a wrathful Father. It is true that as leaders of the little church, we become representatives of God and of
the Church. Let us then be careful to follow the good examples
we are given: let us father like the Father who loves us and who
respects our free will, and let us mother like the All-Holy Theotokos, whose love and compassion know no limits. Let us struggle
to be loving and forgiving, always ready to receive the prodigal by
running to meet him, falling on his neck with kisses.

When you pass through difficult seasons with your kids, know that there are two gifts you were able to give them: you gave them an Orthodox identity, which, even if they reject it, will always be a part of them; and you gave them your example of a good Orthodox life. When you struggled, you turned to God and found strength, and this should give you hope that when your child struggles, she will know she can also turn to God to find strength.

We give our growing children these tremendous gifts freely and sacrificially, and then we wait and pray that God will give them what they need. We must pray for God to fill in for our own weaknesses, and we can trust that He will do so if we are genuinely working to be loving and good parents. Fr. Seraphim Rose said of the Church:

> In only one place is there to be found the fount of true teaching, coming from God Himself, not diminished over the centuries but ever fresh, being one and the same in all those who truly teach it, leading those who follow it to eternal salvation. This place is the Orthodox Church of Christ, the fount is the grace of the All-Holy Spirit, and the true teachers of the Divine doctrine that issues from this fount are the Holy Fathers of the Orthodox Church.

Knowing this as parents gives a great sense of responsibility and importance to our work. Keep at it—no matter what—keep at it!

Think of Abraham and Isaac: God asked Abraham to sacrifice his much-beloved son, and he complied. To our modern minds, far removed from cultures where children were routinely sacrificed, this is a shocking and bizarre request; but of course, God stays Abraham's hand, indicating that He wants no such sacrifices.

The story teaches us more than God's instruction against

human sacrifice. This narrative speaks to us in our powerlessness and asks us to give our children to God, to trust Him to do what is right for them without concern for ourselves. Imagine your child is suffering and you cannot help—whether the child is sick or struggling, parents are eventually forced to recognize their own limits. Suddenly, we see that only God can help, and that indeed, our child belongs to God. We often forget that we are all God's children first, and parents are merely trusted stewards of His beloved children. When there is something wrong with our children, when they struggle for any reason, we should first pray, "Lord, Your child needs you. Come, Lord."

If we can trust that our children are truly God's and not ours, we need never be exasperated or humiliated by their behavior. We don't have to fear they won't turn out well enough—we need only call upon their Father and ask Him to give them what they need. They are His children, and we must commend them to Him.

> So, let us raise our children in such a way that they can face any trouble, and not be surprised when difficulties come; let us bring them up in the discipline and instruction of the Lord. Great will be the reward in store for us, for if artists who make statues and paint portraits of kings are held in high esteem, will God not bless ten thousand times more those who reveal and beautify His royal image (for man is the image of God)? When we teach our children to be good, to be gentle, to be forgiving (all these are attributes of God), to be generous, to love their fellow men, to regard this present age as nothing, we instill virtue in their souls, and reveal the image of God within them. This, then, is our task: to educate both ourselves and our children in godliness; otherwise what answer will we have before Christ's judgment-seat?
> —St. John Chrysostom[42]

Making Your Way Through the Liturgical Year

In her wisdom, the Church maps out our year, carving it into seasons. Just as the earth passes through its cycle of seasons to experience growth and change, so must our spiritual lives.

While the secular year begins in January, the liturgical year begins in September. There are many simple ways a family can celebrate each feast together and start to connect parish and family life in their little church. We have compiled a list of activities you and your family can peruse for inspiration and to help you start the process of celebrating and commemorating the times of the Church Year. We have also developed a Pinterest board at https://www.pinterest.com/orthoblueprints. You'll find activities and projects organized through the Great Feasts, Pascha, and the entire liturgical year.

Attend Divine Liturgy

The best way for any family to engage the feasts of the Church is to make sure they take time from their calendar for the liturgy (and vigil if there is one) to honor the feast. For many families, this may be challenging if work schedules are prohibitive. Others will be able to plan these dates in advance and get a partial time-off from work. It is essential to developing your little church that church attendance increase beyond once a week, and these great feasts are the perfect time to attend weekday services.

Learn the Troparion and Kontakion for the Feast

This is not as tricky as it may seem. Even if your family isn't particularly musical, the texts for these special hymns are easily practiced and learned. This fantastic teaching tool will help instill in all your children the Church teachings about the significance of each feast for our salvation. Remember that we gather information from the whole Tradition—not just bits and pieces. You might invest in a recording of the festal hymns that's appropriate to your tradition (that is, Greek-style or Slavonic-style, etc.) Artists like Khouria Gigi Shadid and Eikona have recorded albums for children featuring the hymns of important feasts. Especially for a family without much musical skill, playing these recordings can make learning the hymns much easier.

Something the Shoemaker family has tried for several years with varied success is to practice and memorize each Troparion and Kontakion for the great feasts. We have endeavored to practice each hymn during our prayer times in the week leading up to the feast's Divine Liturgy. This has not always been successful in our house, but it's always rewarding to watch the children singing with confidence during this part of the Divine Liturgy on feast days. The sheet music for these hymns isn't hard to come by, and it's something our oldest children have always enjoyed making part of our family prayer time. —Caleb

For each feast, the most important thing to do is to communicate the story to your children. You can look up the feasts on any jurisdiction's official website to find the explanation of the events celebrated and their significance. At prayer time or dinner time, story-time or bedtime, teach your children the story and sing the hymns of the feast.[43]

In our house, telling the story of the feast has become a beautiful tradition. In the early years, I was narrating to my children, but as time has passed and the children have grown (and multiplied), the older children have begun to interrupt and tell the stories themselves. When we celebrate feasts, we aren't just remembering an historic event, but we are reliving it and taking in the experience ourselves. A good, exciting story—and a narrator who urges us to find ways in which this is relevant to our lives—makes a big impression and

> *will suffice for those who are not naturally crafty.*
> —*Elissa*

Some children love to play-act stories and will enjoy putting on a puppet show or a skit that teaches the story right back to you. Some children can spend hours lovingly creating paper dolls or felt puppets of the characters, while others prefer to throw together a show in an instant. If your family enjoys such activities, this is a memorable and exciting way to bring the feasts to life in your household.

Nativity of the Most Holy Theotokos (Sept. 8 NC/21 OC)

The first feast of the liturgical year celebrates the birth of Mary, Mother of God. This feast offers a wonderful opportunity to teach about the grandparents of our Lord—for His Incarnation means that like all of us, He had grandparents and a larger family.

Tradition teaches us that Mary's parents, Joachim and Anna, wanted very much to have a child and prayed powerfully for one. They were visited separately by the Archangel Gabriel announcing that they would give birth to Mary, whom Joachim and Anna promised to dedicate to God in the temple.

Before being visited by the Archangel Gabriel, Anna prayed in her garden, weeping bitterly for her barrenness. Sitting under a laurel tree, she saw a nest of sparrows and lamented that while the birds had babies, she did not. In honor of Anna's prayer, children can make and decorate beautiful birds' nests.

At craft and hobby stores, you can buy little nests and decorative birds—or the children can make them from scratch.

NEST

» Stems and leaves, moss, round rocks for eggs

» String or florist's wire

» glue

To make a bird's nest, go into your garden or to a park or trail to locate a plant with long, flexible stems. Collect straw, long vines, or bendable stems, as well as some attractive small leaves and bits of moss.

Work a handful of stems into a U-shape. If possible, weave them together so they'll hold, or simply tie them into place with string or wire. Continue working the stems until they form a ring.

If the nest isn't holding together well, use glue to keep the stems in place.

If the stems are too fresh and keep falling apart, tie the nest together and then hang it to dry so it will dry in the rounded shape.

Decorate your nest with the small leaves and moss and add any egg-like rocks you've found.

BIRDS

Families with origami skills might make origami birds, or those who know how to do felting might create lovely little sparrows for their nests.

For younger children, consider folding a paper plate in half and stapling or gluing it along the round edge to create a rounded little birdy shape. Then allow the children to color the plate and glue on a googly eye.

You might also simply cut bird shapes from cardstock, adding the following fancy options:

» Fold a rectangular piece of paper into an accordion fold, and then cut a slit (the same width as your folded paper) in the paper bird body; slide the folded paper into the slit and open it up to create wings.

» Paint a wooden clothespin and glue it to the back of your bird, so that the feet can be clipped onto the nest.

» Decorate the bird with real feathers.

PRAYERFULNESS

This feast highlights the great prayerfulness of our Lord's grandparents, Joachim and Anna. Here at the beginning of the liturgical year is a good day to spruce up the family prayer corner with the children. You might clean out the shelves, allowing the children to dust and polish (and discuss) the various items you keep there.

In addition, we might allow the children to create little prayer books, either copying down or printing up the prayers of your family prayer rule and binding them into little books (by stapling or tying pages)—one for each family member, with perhaps a few extras for guests.

The Universal Exaltation (Elevation) of the Cross (September 14/27)

The Exaltation of the Cross celebrates the finding of the True Cross by St. Helena, mother of St. Constantine. This is a fantastic opportunity to discuss with your children the importance and significance of the Cross in Orthodox spirituality. This is one of three feasts dedicated to the Cross and a special time for families to focus their attention on the coming year with its fasts and feasts.

Tradition teaches us that when Empress Helena sought the Holy Cross, she found it buried beneath a huge mound of flowering basil. The Patriarch of Jerusalem then raised up ("elevated" or "exalted") the Cross before the faithful. What began as an instrument of pain and humiliation was transformed by our Lord into an instrument of salvation, granting eternal life.

FLOWERING CROSS

This is a project that can be altered depending on the ages of your children. Very young children may be better served by using soft foam or paper rather than wood or florist's shears.

» Wooden cross
» Flowers (real or silk)
» Florist's tape
» Shears or scissors
» Glue gun (optional)

A few days before the feast, place the plain cross in a prominent place in your icon corner. Then, on the eve of the feast (perhaps before or after attending vigil), lay the cross on a table and arrange the flowers on its surface. Use the florist's tape to adhere the flowers to the cross and secure with hot glue gun.

Display this cross in your icon corner throughout the week of the feast.

Optional project for younger children: Cut out paper flowers from construction paper to decorate your family cross.

TOOTHPICK CROSS

This is a great project for elementary and older children and can be made as intricately as the children like.

- » Black construction paper
- » White glue
- » Toothpicks (multicolored preferred)
- » Scissors

Trace and cut out a cross from the construction paper. Glue toothpicks to decorate the cross.

For older or more advanced children, bisect the vertical and horizontal beams of the cross and lay the toothpicks out in a houndstooth or crosshatch pattern.

The Entrance (Presentation) of the Theotokos into the Temple (November 21/December 4)

As Joachim and Anna had prayerfully promised to the Archangel Gabriel, when Mary was three years old they presented her at the temple to be dedicated to God and raised in the temple community.

Members of the family and of the local community gathered together and walked to the Temple with Mary, holding candles and singing the Psalms in a glorious and joyful procession. Mary—only three years old—was so excited that she ran up the steps of the temple to the High Priest Zacharias (father of John the Forerunner) without any help at all. Once inside the temple, the High Priest took Mary into the Holy of Holies, where no one was allowed to enter, and where she would be fed by angels as she grew up.

You might want to form a similar procession in your own home—perhaps singing and processing around the house to finish at the steps of the home or processing inside.

This feast is a good time to talk about what the temple in Jerusalem looked like. You might make a drawing or model of the front of the temple, with its steps for Mary to clamber up, or you might make a model of the temple's interior layout, with the Holy of Holies to house her.

TEMPLE & HOLY OF HOLIES

Create a model of the temple that includes the Holy of Holies, or make only the Holy of Holies itself. You can use whatever materials your family enjoys most—play dough, clay, recycled cardboard boxes, Legos, wooden building blocks, graham crackers—the possibilities are endless. The model need not be beautiful (unless your children love to make beautiful models). It is enough to arrange the food on your plate like a temple to show the little ones where the Holy of Holies would be.

UP THE TEMPLE STEPS

- » cardstock or cardboard from an old cereal box or shoebox
- » pens, pencils, or crayons
- » scissors
- » glue
- » popsicle stick

Draw the temple on a piece of cardstock or cardboard salvaged from an old box. You should see the temple steps running up one side to the temple on the other. Cut a slit along the diagonal of the steps.

Draw the Theotokos on paper or cardstock, color her, and cut her out. Glue her to a popsicle stick to make a nice little puppet.

Slip the popsicle stick into the slit so the Theotokos can run up the stairs.

Optional: Add Joachim and Anna and the High Priest Zacharias. If you'd like, you can print up an icon of the Entrance, then color and cut out the people from the icon for use in your temple scene.

Nativity Fast (November 15/28 through December 24/ January 6)

For forty days before Nativity (Christmas), we prepare our hearts to receive our Lord. As we lead our children in this process, let's ask how Joseph and Mary prepared to receive Him and look to the manger as our model.

When Herod called for the census, Joseph and Mary headed for Bethlehem to be counted. Mary was "great with child" and would be giving birth soon, but they made their way to Bethlehem, probably concerned about exactly how they were going to safeguard this very special baby. They arrived to find the town offered no place for God's Son. Every room was taken. Eventually, Joseph and Mary found space among the livestock; the earth itself offered Him a cave, in which Joseph and Mary prepared to receive our Lord.

Whenever a new baby is coming, the family usually prepares cozy beds and readies stacks of baby clothes and blankets. We want the new baby to know that he is welcome and loved, that he has a special place in this family he's joining. Bethlehem prepared no place for Baby Jesus, but the earth opened itself up and offered Him a warm cave, and Joseph and Mary prepared the manger as best they could.

As Christmas approaches, we prepare our homes by decorating trees and hanging stockings. Let's also prepare our hearts for

Him, making our hearts soft and warm and ready for Jesus to be born again inside of us and to make His home there.

> "I shall give you a new heart and put a new spirit within you. I shall take the heart of stone from your flesh and give you a heart of flesh." (Ezek. 36:26)

How can we transform our hearts so that they are soft and warm? We can pray and fast and be charitable, so that our hearts might be cleansed and grow soft and warm to welcome our Lord.

COTTON BALL MANGER

Younger children can visualize the preparation of a soft place for Jesus by creating a little manger out of a box and then slowly filling it with cotton balls every day, as they mark a good deed done for each day of the fast.

» box (size to hold about 40 cotton balls)
» cotton balls
» brown paper
» pens
» glue

Each child should cover a box in brown paper to make the box begin to look like a manger. Children might decorate the manger realistically, making it look like an item you'd find among livestock, or they could cover it with gold crosses so that it appears more like a liturgical item, or they can choose to decorate it in a Christmas theme, with perhaps a little icon of the Nativity, etc.

Give each child a bag of 40 cotton balls.

Throughout the fast, every day the family can discuss what special thing they did to prepare their hearts today (fasting, praying, scriptural study, charitable actions). Each child can place a cotton ball in his or her manger so that by the time the Nativity arrives, they have prepared a soft place for Baby Jesus.

St. Nicholas (December 6/19)

St. Nicholas was a vivacious, generous, and kind-hearted priest from the city of Patara (who eventually became bishop of Myra). Once in Patara, a poor man had three daughters but had no money for their dowries. (In those days, a girl could not marry without a dowry and could not support herself outside of marriage.) In despair, the man made plans to sell his daughters as slaves. St. Nicholas knew this, and as each girl came of age, he quietly approached the window of their home in the middle of the night, tossing a bag of gold coins into a stocking hung up to dry by the fire to serve as her dowry. Each girl was able to marry a good Christian man and live an honorable life. The holy saint offered this generous gift in secret, reminding us that anonymous charity is more pure and beautiful than efforts to seek fame for oneself.

St. Nicholas is celebrated throughout the Orthodox world as a patron of children, mariners, travelers, pawnbrokers, (repentant) thieves, the wrongly accused, and a host of other special needs and intentions. It's hard to find an Orthodox parish that doesn't have an icon (or two or three) of St. Nicholas on display. His story is beautiful, his intercessions are powerful, and his example for children is incomparable.

SHOES FOR ST. NICHOLAS

Throughout Europe and the Americas, children celebrate St. Nicholas as the bringer of treats and sweets. Much like the American practice of leaving a stocking out for St. Nicholas to fill, European children leave a shoe near the door of the house with a small present for St. Nicholas and receive treats in return.

This can be a welcome alternative to the "naughty-or-nice" retribution of Santa Claus that so permeates our culture. Your children pay a kindness to St. Nicholas (namely, leaving a small treat for him or his horse/camel/donkey, such as a few carrots or some straw), and he repays their kindness with a small blessing. Traditional treats for St. Nicholas to leave behind include nuts, dried fruit, chocolate "gold" coins, oranges (a traditional symbol of St. Nicholas), cookies, or a small religious item such as an icon.

TREATS AND SWEETS

St. Nicholas Day is always commemorated with lots of treats and sweets. You might consider combining the secular tradition of a cookie exchange or ornament swap with your St. Nicholas Day festivities. If you enjoy the idea of throwing a neighborhood (or parish) gathering to exchange Christmas ornaments or holiday goodies, you might consider making it a St. Nicholas Day event so that the festivities become a celebration of this wonderful saint.

GIVING IN SECRET

You might talk with your children about the merits and joys of giving in secret and create an improved Secret Santa type of game, where the children draw names and try to do secret, helpful favors for one another. Rather than simply buying gifts, they can secretly clean up each other's messes, fix broken toys, or find creative and anonymous ways to bring one another joy.

The Nativity of Our Lord Jesus Christ (Christmas) (December 25/January 7)

One of the year's most popular feasts, the Nativity or Christmas, celebrates the birth of Jesus Christ in the flesh—His Incarnation. This feast is marked by Christ's humility, both in that He would take on human flesh at all, and especially in that He came to us as a poor infant from an unremarkable town rather than choosing the splendor of wealth and earthly glories. This makes it so much more painful and ironic that Western celebrations of Christmas have become so focused on excessive gift-giving and consumerism.

It hardly seems necessary to offer an explanation of how to celebrate Christmas, but perhaps we all need help reducing the focus on secular celebration and gift-giving. By fasting and attending church services, by talking about the Nativity story with our children, by focusing our decorations on icons instead of snowmen, we can bring our family's experience of Nativity back to the holy celebration it is meant to be.

Most families have a host of wonderful Christmas traditions. The tradition of decorating our homes with Christmas trees has been baptized, as we say, into the Church, and many Orthodox families will display beautiful trees that feature little icon ornaments made by their children.

ICON ORNAMENTS

You can find blank ornaments at craft stores, or you can simply cut shapes from cardboard and paint them, poking a hole in the top and running string through for a hanger. You can print up color icons or obtain colored icon cards (perhaps cutting them out of last year's church calendar) and glue them onto ornaments, surrounding them with glitter glue, plastic gemstones, and painted designs.

GINGERBREAD NATIVITY SCENE

There's a fun American tradition of decorating gingerbread houses at Christmas time, but this doesn't seem to have much to do with the birth of our Lord. Why not take this secular tradition and bring it to life by creating a beautiful manger scene out of gingerbread and candies? Rather than attempt a house shape, think more about barn shapes. (Tradition tells us Jesus was actually born in a cave, but that would be difficult to build from gingerbread.) Bake your gingerbread in large rectangles and let the kids design their own creche.

If you're not a gingerbread baker, consider sitting the kids down at the table with graham crackers and frosting for their building materials.

You'll want enough people-type figures to create Mary, Joseph, and baby Jesus, an ox and a donkey, angels, three wise men, shepherds, and sheep. Once they're decorated with frosting and candy, you'll be able to tell who is who.

St. Basil (January 1/14)

St. Basil the Great was one of the greatest Fathers of the Church. He came from a holy family and was the first person in human history to establish an orphanage for children and a Christian hospital. His intelligence, generosity, and practical applications of our beautiful faith have brought him great fame and reverence.

St. Basil had a wonderful strategy for helping the poor without compromising their dignity: He asked the women of the Church to bake loaves of wonderful sweet bread with coins hidden inside and pass out the bread to hungry people, who would then find the coins when they broke the bread with their families.

In honor of St. Basil, many Orthodox people bake Vasilopita (Basil bread) on his feast day. This sweet bread with a coin inside is cut into many pieces, and each portion of the Vasilopita is distributed—one for our Lord Jesus Christ, one for the Holy Theotokos, a third for St. Basil, and other portions for the members of the family, beginning with the eldest. In a parish setting, portions may be cut for the various ministries of the Church, for the little church households, the traveler, the visitor, and the poor.

Note that the coins are wrapped in wax paper before baking.

BAKE BREAD WITH COINS INSIDE

You might search online for a Vasilopita recipe (or you might bake your favorite bread with coins inside). You can cut the bread, offering a piece for each of the groups mentioned above. The one who receives the coin is promised God's blessings in the new year.

A particularly beautiful alternative would be to do what St. Basil did: bake several loaves of fresh bread with money inside and pass them out to hungry people you meet on the streets.

CLEAN OUT YOUR CLOSETS

St. Basil said, "When someone steals another's clothes, we call them a thief. Should we not give the same name to one who could clothe the naked and does not? The bread in your cupboard belongs to the hungry; the coat unused in your closet belongs to the one who needs it; the shoes rotting in your closet belong to the one who has no shoes; the money which you hoard up belongs to the poor."

He has a good point—all those clothes in your closet that you are not using could well be put to good use by someone without clothes. Make a family tradition of combing through closets and donating extra shoes and garments to those in need. Honor St. Basil's memory by sharing your bounty with someone who could use another shirt.

The Theophany (Epiphany) of Our Lord Jesus Christ (January 6/19)

When our Lord was baptized in the River Jordan, the Holy Spirit descended upon Him in the form of a dove, and a voice from heaven declared, "This is My beloved Son, in whom I am well pleased." We call our Lord's baptism the Theophany ("revelation of God") because the Holy Trinity revealed itself to us in all three parts at once—the Father's voice, the Son in the flesh, and the Holy Spirit in the form of a dove.

We understand that when we are baptized the water cleanses us from our sins, but when Jesus (who had no sins to wash away) was baptized, something else happened: The holiness of Jesus Christ surged into the river, cleansing and blessing the waters. Imagine His grace flowing into the River Jordan and the river flowing into the sea—so Christ's holiness flowed with it, mixing with all the water on the Earth to sanctify all water and all creation. Those children who have learned the water cycle already know the earth's water is a closed system—we do not gain new water but instead cycle through all the existing water. The water

on Earth today is the same water Jesus Christ stepped into, blessing and sanctifying it with His holiness.

On Theophany, priests all over the world perform the Blessing of the Waters, blessing vessels of water to be passed out to
the faithful and blessing bodies of water such as rivers, lakes, and
oceans. Jesus' sanctification of the waters is repeated every year.
Imagine how many times a single drop of water may have been
blessed in the last two thousand years!

WATER DEMONSTRATION
Try this visual demonstration of God's grace flowing through
water: Fill a clear glass container with clean water. Add food coloring, colored liquid, or milk to it and watch the colored liquid
slowly mix into the waters—just as Christ's holiness has sanctified
all the waters of the Earth.

HOLY WATER BOTTLES
This is the time of year to obtain holy water in your parish. Bring
home a few bottles to keep in your icon corner for use throughout the year. The parish will probably provide small glass or plastic bottles, which you can invite your children to decorate and
personalize. They might glue crosses, icons, or plastic gemstones
onto bottles, decorating them for the glory of God.

3-D ICON DIORAMA
The icon of Theophany is a particularly engaging one, with a
lot of activity going on. Build a diorama to bring it to life in your
home.

» box
» paper
» glue
» string
» pens or crayons
» tissue paper
» popsicle sticks

Select a box and create the background. You can glue blue paper on the top for sky and green or brown paper in the background for the wilderness.

You'll want to use blue tissue paper (or perhaps use watercolors to turn white tissue paper blue) to create the river on the base of the box. Crunch up the paper so it has a lot of texture, and then put large dots of glue all over the bottom of the box. Glue the paper irregularly to the bottom so there are big waves indicating the wildness of the water when it changed course.

Make colorful fish by drawing them on paper, coloring them, and cutting them out. Glue them into the river so they are jumping wildly.

Make a dove out of white paper to be the Holy Spirit. Pop a hole in the roof of the box and tie the dove with a string so it hangs in air above Jesus.

You might make a quotation bubble for God the Father's declaration, "This is my beloved Son, in whom I am well pleased." Hang this from the roof as well.

Draw Jesus and John the Baptist—or, if you prefer, print up a copy of the icon—and cut out the figures, coloring them in. Glue popsicle sticks along their backs, and then cut slits in the base of the box so you can stand them upright in the scene.

The Meeting of Our Lord Jesus Christ in the Temple (February 2/15)

On the fortieth day of his life, as was the custom under the Jewish Law, Joseph and Mary brought baby Jesus to the temple. Jesus is both fully human and fully God; and as a true human being, He was subject to the Law.

There was an old man named Simeon who loved God very much. God promised him he would see the Messiah before he died, and when he saw Mary enter the temple with the baby Jesus, he recognized Him and said,

"Lord, now You are letting Your servant depart in peace,
According to Your word;
For my eyes have seen Your salvation
Which You have prepared before the face of all peoples,
A light to *bring* revelation to the Gentiles,
And the glory of Your people Israel." (Luke 2:29–32)

We sing this prayer at every Vespers service, celebrating that we, like Simeon, have been blessed with the presence of our Savior.

Candles are traditionally blessed on this day.

EASY BEESWAX CANDLES
   » sheets of beeswax
   » long wicks

Invite your children to lay a wick at the edge of a sheet of beeswax, and then roll it up. This will create a lovely beeswax candle to be used in your prayer corner.

Beeswax sheets also make beautiful ornaments to hang in the window. Use your cookie cutters to cut shapes out of the beeswax sheets and then stack them—including a small amount of white glue and a small ribbon loop tucked in between—to create a lovely little hanging ornament.

The Annunciation to the Most Holy Theotokos (March 25/April 7)

In the Garden of Eden, Eve was asked not to touch the fruit that would bring death, but Eve said no, choosing instead to direct her own fate and to plunge mankind into its fall, making human beings subject to death. Many years later, an angel came to Mary and asked her to bear mankind's Savior, and Mary said yes.

This feast celebrates the archangel's announcement to Mary that she would soon bear the Son of God, and her immediate and complete assent.

In saying yes, Mary reverses the old curse and becomes the New Eve, who aligns her own will with God's will and becomes the Mother of God. This is a good opportunity to discuss the ways in which we might say yes to God in our own lives, enabling our own salvation and becoming His hands and feet in this world.

YES JOURNAL
- » cardstock
- » paper
- » bamboo skewer (or another straight stick)
- » rubber band
- » hole punch

Cut 8½" x 8½" squares of the paper and cardstock—two of cardstock for covers and as many as you like of paper for the inside pages.

Punch two holes in each page (paper and cardstock). Stack the pages with cardstock on the front and back.

Cut the skewer to 8". Poke a rubber band through one hole, and put the skewer through it. Poke the other end of the rubber band through the other hole, and catch it on the skewer as well.

Invite children to write in the journal about the various ways they might plan to say yes to God, and then to continue writing entries over time as they find opportunities to say yes.

For younger children, a more concrete craft might be more appropriate. You might make angels to commemorate Archangel Gabriel's visit to the Theotokos.

ANGEL

- » cupcake-sized baking cups
- » ½" or 1" pompoms
- » white glue
- » scissors

Fold one baking cup into the skirts of the angel's robe, and either fold or cut arms from another baking cup. Glue the wings onto the body, and glue a pompom for the angel's head.

Forgiveness Sunday

On the eve of Great Lent, most Orthodox traditions hold a Forgiveness Vespers, in which the faithful ask forgiveness from one another ("Forgive me, a sinner!") and offer it in return ("May God forgive us both!"). If attending the Vespers is not an option—or perhaps, when you return home from Vespers—it makes sense that the little church would observe the same practice. Family life gives rise to plenty of opportunities for frustration and anger, and it's important that we teach our children to ask and to offer forgiveness. As the prayer of St. Ephraim will remind us throughout the season, we must learn to see our own sins and not to judge our brothers and sisters. Great Lent is best begun with this humble, clean slate.

FORGIVENESS DEMONSTRATIONS

Some children learn best when an idea is demonstrated visually. We can "show" forgiveness using clear glasses of water:

» 1 fizzy tablet per person (Alka-Seltzer, etc.)
» 1 clear glass of water per person

Each person holds a glass of clean, clear water. Hold up the tablets, and note that they are solid and hard. The tablets signify an injury or offense someone might do to you, a solid harm and pain. If we wish to forgive that injury, we might lift it up in prayer to God. Drop the tablets into the glasses of water, which represent God's mercy. As we pray that God helps us forgive, He begins to dissolve those pains and injuries so that they disappear (not instantly, but slowly and through prayer and participation in the life of the Church). Note that the water may be different after the tablets dissolve, just as we might be changed by our experiences.

GOD FORGIVES US

» 1 glass of water per person
» icon of Christ
» food coloring with droppers
» bleach with droppers

In this case, each glass of water represents our own heart. We can hold the glass in front of the icon of Christ and see Him clearly.

When we sin (drop in some food coloring), we cloud the water and make it harder to see the icon of Christ clearly (the colors are all wrong, etc.). If we ask for forgiveness, God can forgive our sins—He can cleanse us and make us clean again (drop in some bleach). Now we can once again properly see the icon of Christ. (Be sure not to let the children drink the bleached water!)

Great Lent

As Great Lent approaches, take time to work out how the fast will be observed by each child. You might print up a page divided by a cross into four sections: Prayer, Alms, Study, and Fasting. In each quadrant, the child can, after thoughtful and prayerful consideration, write the particular way in which he or she will observe this important aspect of Great Lent. Like a prayer rule, this will become the fasting rule for that child.

For those who cannot enter into the full fast, this is an opportunity to find a lesser fast that will be a love offering without over-taxing them. The worksheet invites reflection not just on the food aspect of the fast, but also on how each child might increase her almsgiving, religious study, and prayer life. Post the completed worksheets inside a pantry or cupboard door or near the icon corner, so the children can remind themselves of the offering they hoped to make—so they can better fulfill those worthy goals.

For younger children, it is often helpful to invent a variation on an Advent calendar to help them mark the forty days of Lent and to remind them to do good deeds every day in preparation for Pascha. You might use a traditional calendar, marking Forgiveness Sunday and Holy Pascha, and let them cross out each day— asking themselves at the end of each day what they have done that day to observe the fast and to prepare for the Resurrection.

If you prefer, you might look up an old Greek tradition called *Kyra Sarakosti* or Lady Lent. This is a cookie you can bake that looks like a lady with no mouth (because she's fasting), whose hands are folded in prayer and who has seven (yes, seven!) feet— one for each Sunday of Great Lent. Every week, you remove one of her feet to count down to Holy Pascha.

CLEAN MONDAY (FIRST DAY OF GREAT LENT)

On the first day of Great Lent, most Orthodox will offer a particularly strict fast to prepare themselves for the long haul that precedes Pascha. We hope to be cleansed of our sins during the fast, and so we begin with literal cleansing: our diet is "clean," and in many traditions, we take this week to thoroughly clean our houses as well (think of spring cleaning with a spiritual element).

Parents may choose to take their children on a nature walk on Clean Monday. This allows a natural opportunity for conversation about the purpose of the fast and lends itself to observations about the difficulties of modern distractions. Quiet in God's creation, we naturally find we are closer to God when the gadgets and televisions are far behind us. This sets us up for a successful and thoughtful fast.

ST. THEODORE SATURDAY (FIRST SATURDAY OF GREAT LENT) & SATURDAYS OF SOULS (THROUGHOUT THE FAST AND THE LITURGICAL YEAR)

Tradition teaches that the Emperor Julian the Apostate (around AD 362) knew that Christians would be hungry after the first week of strict fasting and would head to Constantinople's marketplaces on Saturday to buy food. Thinking himself very clever, he ordered the blood of pagan sacrifices to be sprinkled over all the food in the markets so that Christians would be forced to break their fast.

St. Theodore the Tyro appeared in a dream to Patriarch Eudoxios, warning him of the plot. He told him to ask all the Christians not to buy any food, but instead to boil the wheat (*koliva*) they had at home and eat it sweetened with honey. As a result, this first Saturday of Great Lent has come to be known as Theodore Saturday. After the service, koliva is distributed to all who are present.

Koliva has become connected with celebrating the memory of those who have fallen asleep in the Lord, for Jesus said, "Most assuredly, I say to you, unless a grain of wheat falls into the ground and dies, it remains alone; but if it dies, it produces much grain" (John 12:24). In recognition that our falling asleep is really just a planting, that our eternal lives are only just beginning, the Orthodox faithful make koliva and bless it at memorial services. This is a beautiful, prayerful offering that reminds us of the real connection we continue to experience with our loved ones who die before us.

On Theodore Saturday or at any time of the year, especially on an anniversary of the falling asleep of someone you know or on a Saturday of Souls throughout Great Lent and the Pascha season, we might take the opportunity to teach our children how to make koliva. When a beloved family member or friend passes away, children in particular feel better when there is something they can do to help. Making koliva is an excellent job for them when families are grieving.

Every family and every region has a variation on the koliva recipe, so we offer two different recipes, as they are our own ways of making koliva—surely you'll find your own way that works for you and your family. The important thing is to prepare sweetened, boiled wheat. People have been known to include white chocolate chips or the favorite candies of the deceased—if it's sweet, you are free to add it and to develop your own koliva tradition. Many people will add spices, or they'll bring in some color with green accents of chopped parsley or mint, or fresh red accents from pomegranate seeds or dried cranberries.

Note that making koliva is not like baking prosphora (communion bread), where there are hard and fast rules regarding how to make it right; for koliva, the most important thing is that grain is used, because of the symbolism surrounding Christ's words.

Caleb's recipe

- » 1 c. dry wheat berries (approx. 4 c. cooked)
- » 1 c. raisins
- » 1/3 c. brown sugar
- » ½ c. walnuts
- » cinnamon and mint to taste
- » powdered sugar

Cook the wheat berries according to the directions, drain, and cool. Store in the fridge overnight (this will help the drying process). In a large mixing bowl, place cooked wheat berries, brown sugar, raisins, and walnuts. Mix well. Add cinnamon and mint according to your preference. Transfer from bowl to a serving dish (pie plate, platter, casserole). Sift powdered sugar over the

entire mixture until the berries are all covered and white. Decorate with nuts, Jordan almonds, fruit, berries, etc. in the shape of
a cross.

Note: Many Greek grandmotherly types say that if you'd like
to keep the white powdered sugar looking flawless for presentation, you might first cover the koliva with a layer of finely ground
graham cracker dust, toasted flour, or ground zwieback dust to
provide a liquid-absorbing layer so that no moisture will affect
the look of the white powdered-sugar layer.

Elissa's recipe

  - » 1 c. dry wheat berries (approx.. 4 c. cooked)
  - » ½ c. brown sugar
  - » ¼ c. white sugar
  - » 1 tsp. salt
  - » 3 Tbsp. cinnamon
  - » 2 Tbsp. cumin
  - » 1 tsp. coriander
  - » 1 c. chopped almonds
  - » 1 c. chopped pecans
  - » 1 c. whole pecans

The night before the memorial, place dried wheat berries into a
saucepan and cover with water. Bring to a boil, cover, and remove
from heat. After half an hour, add 2 more cups boiling water. Let
sit, covered. Before bed, drain wheat berries and lay them out on
a large towel or cookie sheet to dry overnight.

In the morning, place wheat berries in a large mixing bowl,
add the rest of the ingredients, and mix well. Place koliva in an
attractive bowl and make a cross on top with the whole pecans.

Make sure to call your priest if you plan to bring koliva to a service so that he is prepared to bless it and to offer memorial prayers for your loved ones. Prepare a list of deceased people to commemorate; you can offer a memorial for a particular person (perhaps on an anniversary of their passing), or you can offer a list of names (split into Orthodox and non-Orthodox for the priest's guidance) to commemorate together in one service. After the memorial prayers, the blessed koliva should be shared with the entire congregation.

Lazarus Saturday

As we approach Pascha, the Church celebrates the various events of our Lord's final days, entering into those days and experiencing them anew.

After the forty days of Great Lent, we come to Lazarus Saturday, in which we celebrate the day Christ brought His friend back to life after four days in the tomb. This glorious feast celebrates the resurrection-before-the-Resurrection, announcing Christ's victory over death even before Pascha.

The story is told in John 11:1–45: After delaying His arrival, Christ approaches Lazarus's tomb and calls out, "Lazarus, come out!" His friend miraculously comes forth from the tomb, bound with the strips of burial cloth, and Jesus says, "Unbind him, and let him go." Christ calls out for Lazarus to do something (come out) and for the community to assist him (unbind him)—His miracle, as is so often true, requires our effort in conjunction with His grace.

This is an excellent opportunity to think with our children about how our sins bind us and how we, as a community, can

help to unbind one another. We might create little Lazarus figures (who resemble ourselves) out of popsicle sticks or pipe cleaners and bind them up with our own sins—each of them written on
a slip of white paper and wrapped on the figure as grave-clothes.
Only when we and our community work together to extricate
ourselves from sin can we truly be born into new life.

Greek tradition offers *Lazarakia*, a traditional cookie made to
look like a little Lazarus figure wrapped in grave-clothes.

Palm Sunday (The Entrance of Our Lord Jesus Christ into Jerusalem)

After the resurrection of Lazarus, in which our Lord demonstrated His great power over death, Jesus entered Jerusalem for
the final time. In fulfillment of the prophecies, He processed into
Jerusalem on the colt of a donkey, and the people came out to
meet Him waving palm branches, crying, "Hosanna! Blessed is
He that comes in the Name of the Lord, the King of Israel!"

In parishes across the world, the Orthodox will fold palm
leaves into crosses and other beautiful shapes to mark this great
feast. (In some places where palms do not commonly grow, other
plants such as pussy willows will replace them.)

Holy Week

As the Church approaches Pascha, the services intensify, and so
should our observances within the family. The Orthodox experience of Holy Week and Pascha teaches the entire story of our
salvation, so we should take special care to make sure our children are understanding the narrative of these days, and most

especially, the harrowing of Hades and the Resurrection of Jesus Christ.

HOLY MONDAY AND TUESDAY: BRIDEGROOM SERVICES
Church services on these holy days focus on being ready and watchful, vigilant, for the coming of our Lord. We speak of Christ as the coming Bridegroom, who will join His Bride, the Church, at the Great & Holy Pascha to come (both this Pascha for which we prepare ourselves, and the eventual and final Pascha, the end of days when we are finally and permanently united to our Lord).

Our services speak of the Parable of the Ten Virgins, told in Matthew 25. Read the parable with your children, and discuss the idea that the ten virgins (all of us) are awaiting the coming of our Lord—we don't know exactly when He'll arrive, but we want to be ready to join Him. The oil the virgins carry in their lamps represents the works that should accompany our faith. Without this oil—these works—we will not be ready to accompany the Bridegroom when He comes.

Holy Monday and Holy Tuesday would be well spent trimming or making an oil lamp. Olive oil lampadas are simple enough to create and make for a beautiful visual demonstration of the days' important central theme.

Olive oil lampada
   » glass container or votive holder
   » olive oil
   » cork floater and wick
Load the wick into the cork floater as per instructions. Fill the

glass container two-thirds full of olive oil and place the wick and cork float in the oil. Light the wick.

HOLY WEDNESDAY: HOLY UNCTION & SPIRITUAL HEALING

The Holy Church continues the imagery of oil as mercy and compassion with the service of Holy Unction, which is observed on Holy Wednesday in most Orthodox jurisdictions. In this holy sacrament, we pray for the healing of soul and body and for the forgiveness of sins, and each participant is anointed with oil—for not only (as we learned on Holy Monday and Tuesday) does oil represent our own acts of love and compassion, but oil is God's love and mercy pouring down onto us. Just as the Good Samaritan poured oil on the wounds of the man he found injured on the side of the road, God pours His healing oil over our injuries and ailments.

After the Holy Unction services (perhaps at evening prayers), you might anoint the children with oil from the olive oil lampada, reminding them that oil is mercy and love and healing compassion.

Bandage cross

As we think about the idea of Holy Wednesday's spiritual healing with our kids, we might introduce a craft in which they make crosses out of Band-Aids—either putting down two bandages perpendicular to one another to form a cross on a colorful background, or perhaps covering a cross-shaped piece of paper with bandages.

Prayer for healing

If you have not already started an ongoing list of the sick and suffering servants of God for your prayer corner, today is a good day to begin it. You can simply write it on paper, or you can hang a plate and use dry-erase markers to keep the list up-to-date. You can buy chalkboard paint in one of many colors and paint a square on the wall or on the inside of a cabinet door to accommodate your family's list.

This is also a good time to start teaching your family a prayer for the sick. You might find a short version your kids can memorize, and the family can say it together whenever someone falls ill (or when you drive past an accident on the road or hear an ambulance siren as it zips past). If the full prayer is too much for your family to memorize, consider learning just the first sentence. You can always memorize more later.

HOLY THURSDAY

On Holy Thursday, we commemorate our Lord's washing of the disciples' feet, the institution of the Holy Eucharist at the Mystical Supper, the betrayal of Judas, and Christ's prayers and arrest in the Garden of Gethsemane.

Christ washes the feet of the disciples

We might wash one another's feet in the family on this day, taking turns to sit before one another and humbly cleanse each other with real contact and love. This exercise requires us to be humble enough to touch another's dirty feet and to be vulnerable enough to allow someone else to wash our feet. This opens up an avenue for discussing the idea that we have to be willing both to serve and to be served; asking for help and accepting it can be as difficult as deciding to be the giver of help.

Mystical Supper

Whether you prefer to color an icon line-drawing, make a more elaborate diorama, or even create a reproduction with clay, Barbie dolls, or action figures, asking the kids to make their own version of the icon of the Mystical Supper will bring their attention to its details. We see the Church gathered together in a loving community with Jesus blessing us. Note that Judas reaches for the bread, indicating his betrayal, and that John lays his head on Jesus' chest, indicating that he is the most beloved.

Point out to the children that at every Divine Liturgy, we repeat Christ's words from this evening in the consecration of the Body and Blood.

Create a chalice

Most grocery and party stores sell disposable plastic wine glasses, which make beautiful communion chalice crafts.

> » 1 plastic wine glass per person
> » gold paint
> » glue
> » rhinestones and other decorations

Paint the wine glasses gold. (Spray paint works best, but any gold paint will do. If you have very young children, you might spray the glasses gold first and then give them to the children.)

Decorate the chalice with rhinestones, ribbons, foam crosses, small icons, and any appropriate decorations you have.

GREAT & HOLY FRIDAY

Great and Holy Friday, commemorating the Crucifixion of Jesus Christ, is one of the most solemn days of the year. Most parishes will celebrate services throughout the day, and we encourage you to pull your children from school (write a note announcing a religious holiday) and bring them to church for the services (Royal Hours, Descent from the Cross, Lamentations, etc.). If your parish does not offer a youth retreat on this day, you might talk to your priest about starting one. Children will benefit from seeing the events of Holy Friday as they unfold, and they'll enjoy participating in the decoration of Christ's Tomb.

Decorate the Tomb

Traditionally, each parish has a table that serves as Christ's Tomb which will be covered with flowers on Holy Friday, so that when the clergy lay Jesus in His Tomb it is clearly a life-giving tomb; new life (flowers) springs forth from it. If your children cannot help to decorate the Tomb in the church, you could make one at home.

- » shoebox
- » silk flowers
- » glue

While leaving the edges of the box intact, cut large pieces out of the sides so it resembles the open kouvloukion or tomb (the top and bottom should remain intact, with the top supported by the four vertical edges of the box).

Glue flowers onto the box in whatever pattern or design you prefer.

Optional: Wrap an icon of Christ in white cloth (as Joseph of Arimathea wrapped Jesus' body) and place it in the tomb.

At the foot of the Cross

In the Holy Friday Lamentations, we hear the the hymns of the

Theotokos standing at the foot of the Cross. She contemplates the paradox of Christ's crucifixion: "Today He who hung the earth upon the waters is hung upon the Cross." It is truly amazing that the One who created this earth has been crucified by His own creation. With mature enough children, it is helpful to discuss these themes and to note that when presented with perfect innocence and love, mankind reacts by attacking and killing Him. While we love Jesus, all of us have these tendencies to sometimes react angrily or enviously to goodness. This is a good day to contemplate that and to repent.

As the hymn conjures the image of the Theotokos at the foot of the Cross, the idea of presenting ourselves—of laying our sins and our troubles—at the foot of the Cross is powerful.

» slips of paper

» pens

» Cross (ideally, one with an icon of Jesus on it) or the icon of Extreme Humility

Invite children to write their worries, prayers, or sins on slips of paper and prayerfully set them at the foot of the Cross today. Talk with them about how we bring our broken and contrite hearts as an offering to our Lord, trusting that He will heal us and bring us to abundant life.

GREAT & HOLY SATURDAY

From the time of man's Fall, when man invited death into the world, human beings have been subject to corruption, illness, and injury. Before Christ's Incarnation, when people died, they'd go to Hades, which held good people and bad people together. They were locked behind the gates that held them in Hades, held prisoner by the devil.

When Jesus is hung on a cross on Holy Friday, the devil knows God's own Son is on His way to Hades—and he congratulates himself on having finally conquered Jesus Christ. But God is more powerful than the devil and more powerful than death. Once he is locked into Hades, Jesus Christ rises and breaks open the gates. Hades cannot hold Him. He completely destroys Hades—it doesn't even exist anymore. The people pour out, liberated, and the devil remains there, empty-handed and defeated, as Christ triumphs over him.

Celebrating this holy feast with our families is a profound and beautiful gift. We should teach this story to our children so they can understand the victory we proclaim when we cry out, "Christ is risen!"

We mark Christ's harrowing of Hades on Holy Saturday. Take your children to the liturgy that day and tell them the story. In some parishes, people use noisemakers to mark the event; in others, we simply sing "Arise, O God!" with great joy. However your parish celebrates, be there with your children to mark this first feast of the Resurrection.

Great and Holy Pascha

Whether your parish celebrates at midnight or the next morning, don't be afraid to bring your children to the amazing, long, miraculous Pascha services. In many parishes, the services begin before midnight and continue long into the night, and parents dress their babies and toddlers in pajamas, carrying blankets and pillows in tow. While it may go against our parental instincts to allow our children to stay up so late, understand that Holy Pascha is so enormous, so disruptive, that it must turn the entire world on its head. Don't be afraid to bring your children to midnight services.

SING THE HYMN

At every prayer time—morning and evening, blessings before and after meals—for the forty days following Holy Pascha, sing this joyful hymn with your children. If you can, sing it three times and in different languages. Let this be a truly joyful reminder of the great victory we celebrate.

> *Christ is risen from the dead, trampling down death by death, and upon those in the tombs bestowing life!*

PASCHA BASKETS

Many parishes observe the old Slavic tradition of blessing Pascha baskets. These are baskets of treats that were not allowed during the fast. Families place their baskets in the church, and the priest blesses the reintroduction of these rich, festal foods into the diet. Traditions vary, but Pascha baskets often contain kulich (a Pascha bread), Pascha cheese, ham, butter, sausage, bacon, salt, eggs, and wine. Everything is packed into a basket and covered with a decorated cloth. After the Pascha liturgy, the priest blesses the baskets, and then the families break the fast with these blessed foods.

Families sometimes go well out of their way to reproduce the perfect traditional basket, only to find that their kids don't particularly like kulich and Pascha cheese, and would have preferred ribs and cheesy puffs. Be sure to pack treats for the whole family into your basket. If traditional foods appeal to your family, then by all means, load them into the basket. If you or your children have different tastes, or have really missed some specific foods during the fast, be sure to create a basket full of foods that will provoke great excitement and a joyous breaking of the fast.

You might spend some time thinking about creating a meaningful cloth to cover your basket. If one of your children is interested in needlework, they might embroider a cross onto a cloth during Great Lent, or you might invite the kids to use crayons to decorate a plain cloth and then iron the decorations into the fabric.

RED EGGS

This is a tradition in Orthodoxy that extends back as far as the first century. There are a number of reasons Orthodox Christians dye their eggs red and have them blessed at Pascha. According to the Lives of the Saints, St. Mary Magdalene (who followed our Lord during His earthly ministry and from whom He cast out seven demons) was brought to trial in Rome before the emperor. She proclaimed the Gospel message with boldness and proclaimed the risen Christ to the emperor and his court. According to one version of the story, the emperor laughed at her description of the Resurrection of Christ and told her, "It would be easier for this egg [which he had before him] to turn red." St. Mary is said to have picked up the egg, looked the emperor in the eye, and said, "Just as you say, so let it be." And the egg turned red in her hand.

Eggs have always been a symbol of resurrection. Ancient Egyptians, Babylonians, Greeks, and Romans all used the egg to symbolize life after death and restoration from death and decay. Christians used the common symbol of the resurrection—the popular egg—and dyed it red as part of their Paschal celebrations. This is a fun project for families and a way of uniting your homes not only with other Orthodox around the world, but with Christians throughout time.

This is an easy project to do with your children or with children from your parish, or even as a youth ministry project. A few tips to keep in mind as you prepare for the project:

» White onion skins will produce red dye; red onions, purple

» Older eggs (refrigerated a week or two before boiling) are best for cracking

» This project takes a few days to complete. It is traditional in some jurisdictions to dye eggs on Great and Holy Thursday so they are ready for Pascha liturgy on Saturday night.

It is common practice to play a game with red eggs after liturgy during the agape meal. Two people face each other and greet each other with the Paschal greeting (Christ is risen!/Indeed He is risen!), then try to crack each other's eggs with a single tap. The loser agrees to pray for the winner throughout the year.

Recipe (for home; assume larger quantities for parish celebration)

» The skin of approx. 2 doz. white onions

» Eggs (as many as you want)

» Water

» Olive oil

» Large soup or stock pot

» Wire drying rack

» Paper towel

Directions:

» Place onion skins in stock pot full of water.

» Bring water and skins to a boil and simmer for 20 minutes.

» Carefully place eggs in the pot, trying not to crack the shells.

» Return water, skin, and eggs to a boil and boil for 2–5 minutes.

» Turn off heat and let eggs and water cool on burner.

» If possible, place eggs and dye in the refrigerator overnight.

» Remove eggs from dye and place on wire drying rack to dry.

» Polish eggs with paper towel and olive oil (optional).

Radonitsa or "The Day of Rejoicing": Proclaiming the Good News in the Cemetery (Second Tuesday after Holy Pascha)

On the Tuesday after Thomas Sunday (that is, the second Tuesday after Pascha), in the Slavic tradition, parishioners head out to the cemeteries to sing "Christ is Risen!" to those who lie in the tombs and to pray for the souls of those brothers and sisters who have fallen asleep in the Lord. Our Lord went down into Hades to preach to its inhabitants and break open its gates; we too come out to the tombs to announce the good news of the victory over death to those who have fallen asleep.

Celebrate Radonitsa with your family, singing the good news of Christ's Resurrection to those who lie in the tombs. When we proclaim Christ's victory over death in a place of death, the resurrection becomes so much more real and personal.

The Ascension of Our Lord and Savior Jesus Christ

After His Resurrection, Our Lord appeared to His beloved disciples many times. His body was different after He rose from the dead, for He could appear and disappear and travel through locked doors, but it was still Him—He still carried the marks of His crucifixion, and His disciples knew Him and shared meals with Him. He continued to teach them about the Kingdom of God, and after forty days, He ascended to heaven, taking His risen, human body with Him. He goes to heaven to prepare a place for us and to sit in glory at the right hand of the Father.

CHRIST ASCENDING

Most fun Ascension crafts involve creating a cluster of clouds at the top and a cluster of disciples at the bottom, with a mechanism to move Jesus up from the people to the clouds. Ours uses only paper, but you can be creative and come up with all sorts of ways to show Jesus ascending with string, popsicle sticks, etc. The sky's the limit.

- » paper or cardstock
- » scissors
- » crayons or pens
- » glue
- » cotton balls

Choose a piece of paper or cardstock for the background and cut two slits in the top. Color in a background on this page with the ground at the bottom and the sky at the top. Make clouds in the sky by gluing cotton balls to the upper third of the page, being careful not to glue directly on or above or below the slits. (This is where we'll be pulling Jesus up and down.)

Print up an icon of the Ascension (whether a line-drawing or regular icon) and have the kids cut out the group of disciples, then cut out Jesus separately. Color the disciples and glue them to the background. Color Jesus, but don't attach Him to the page.

Cut a long thin slip of paper (a little narrower than the slits you've cut in the background) and glue it to the back of Jesus' head, so that at least 5 or 6 inches come out above Him. If you've colored the sky, make this slip of paper match it.

Slide the slip connected to Jesus into the slits so that you can pull Him up into the clouds and then bring Him back down to earth. Have fun reenacting our Lord's Ascension!

Pentecost: The Descent of the Holy Spirit

Ten days after our Lord ascended to heaven, just as He'd promised, He sent the Holy Spirit to His disciples. Tongues of fire (flames) appeared on the heads of every apostle. Suddenly, as they witnessed to the Gospel, preaching to people from all corners of the earth, their words reached directly into every heart. Language divisions ceased to matter, so that every person could understand the Gospel message of Jesus Christ, regardless of his mother tongue. The curse of the Tower of Babel was reversed; language was no longer a barrier. Jesus Christ conquers.

TONGUES OF FIRE HEADBAND
A popular craft among Orthodox is the tongues of fire headband—a construction-paper flame (cut from orange or yellow paper) affixed to a construction-paper headband to symbolize the flame of the Holy Spirit sitting on the head of each apostle. This craft invites us to recreate the holy icon of the feast and to

consider whether we are apostles, whether we are ready to be filled with the Holy Spirit and to preach the Gospel as they did.

FRUITS OF THE SPIRIT DOVE MOBILE

From the baptism of Jesus Christ, the Holy Spirit has taken the form of a dove—and on Pentecost, it's a flame. Consider making a dove mobile where small flames hang from a beautiful dove, each representing one of the fruits of the Holy Spirit.

» string
» white paper plate
» glue
» white and orange construction paper

Cut the paper plate in half and affix the two halves together as wings. Cut a bird's head and body from the white paper and glue them to the wings to create a dove.

Cut out flames from the orange paper and write one particular gift or fruit of the Holy Spirit on each: love, joy, peace, long-suffering, kindness, goodness, faithfulness, gentleness, and self-control (Gal. 5:22).

Hang the flames below the dove to create a beautiful Holy Spirit-themed mobile.

Apostles' Fast

Having received the Holy Spirit at Pentecost, we are left with the obvious question: What are we to do with this great blessing? Now we consider the Holy Apostles and what they did with the Holy Spirit.

On the Sunday before the fast begins, we celebrate All Saints Day—recognizing all the unnamed and unknown saints. On this day, we are reminded that saints aren't just famous people living extraordinary lives, but that every ordinary person is called to be a saint too; we are all called to be transformed in our Lord. Like the apostles, a collection of regular people from various walks of life, we are called to pick up our crosses and follow the Lord, to spread the good news of His Resurrection, and to invite Him to transform our hearts.

This fast is a great time to talk with our kids about the twelve holy apostles, telling them what happened to each of them throughout their lives. The apostles received the Holy Spirit and went out into the world, witnessing to the good news of Christ's Resurrection and His victory over death. Our efforts may not be as dramatic as theirs, but when we're willing to talk openly about our Church with the neighbors, classmates, and other people God places in our path, we too are bearing witness.

This is a good time to engage your kids in conversation about exactly how we witness to the One True Faith, how we spread the Gospel of Jesus Christ in our time and place. How have they already done so? What can they do—what can the family do—in the future?

FISHERMAN CRAFT

Our Lord chose simple fishermen and made the fishers of men. If we think about it, this is a perfect choice, because we understand that He chose people who were not already capable of great things. His love and the Holy Spirit transformed them into people who could do amazing things. So we cannot say we are not good enough, strong enough, or smart enough to accomplish this holy work: like the fishermen, we begin simple and weak but open to

Christ's transforming love, which can work wonders through us.

» Saved mesh food packaging bags (such those used for fresh fruits and vegetables)
» construction paper
» popsicle sticks
» scissors
» white glue

Cut out fish and people shapes from construction paper.

Lay a piece of mesh across a sheet of construction paper and lay out a line of glue along the top and bottom. Place a popsicle stick along each line of glue, pressing down.

Slip fish and people inside the net to represent both the fish and the men Christ's fishers of men were able to catch.

Dormition Fast (August 1–14/14–27)

The Dormition fast is roughly two weeks long and affords a perfect opportunity to study the life of the Holy Theotokos with our children.

Our Lord's first miracle, of course, occurred at the behest of His mother, at the wedding in Cana, where the Theotokos observed that the hosts were running out of wine (see John 2:1–11). She mentioned the deficiency to her Son, who reminded her that He was not yet ready to begin His public ministry. The Theotokos, however, told the servants, "Whatever He says to you, do it." Christ instructs the servants to fill the waterpots with water, which miraculously becomes the most wonderful wine. While our Lord had not come to the wedding intending to work wonders, the quiet insistence and intercession of His mother compelled Him to help.

Not only does the Mother of God notice when we have needs, but she quietly presses us to listen to our Lord so that He might fill them. We ask the intercessions of the Mother of God, the Holy Theotokos, that she might see our needs and relay them to our Lord, who always listens to His mother.

WATERPOT CRAFT
  - » clay (which can be baked into a hard form)
  - » small pre-printed icons of the Theotokos
  - » Mod Podge

Allow the children to create little waterpots out of clay. Bake as directed and allow them to paint the pots. Cover the painted pot with a layer of Mod Podge, and while it's wet, smooth the icon of the Theotokos onto the waterpot. After this coat dries, apply more coats of Mod Podge over the entire pot, especially over the icon of the Theotokos.

After it dries, this little waterpot decorated with the icon of the Theotokos will be a wonderful reminder that she is our most fervent intercessor and loves us as our own mothers do.

The Transfiguration of Our Lord God and Savior Jesus Christ (August 6/19)

On this feast, we celebrate the day when our Lord Jesus Christ was transfigured on the mountain, appearing in His divine glory. Our Lord took just three of His disciples to the top of Mt. Tabor with Him. There He revealed Himself in His true and divine glory, robed in white, His face shining forth with uncreated light.

SUNCATCHER

Older children who enjoy complex crafts might recreate the entire icon, while for younger children you might focus simply on making Jesus in glowing white robes.

» wax paper
» a few bottles of white school glue
» food coloring
» paper clips
» *Optional*: cookie cutters and other shapes

Determine what colors you'll want and add food coloring to the glue bottles you'd like to color; cover and shake. Be sure to keep one bottle white.

Lay out a piece of wax paper.

To create images freehand, use one color to outline the drawing, then fill in between the lines with the appropriate glue color.

Create an image of Jesus standing on Mt. Tabor, dressed all in white.

When you are finished, place the paper clip somewhere at the top of your suncatcher so it will dry in place.

Allow to dry for twenty-four hours. Then carefully remove suncatchers from wax paper and hang in your window so sunlight can shine through them.

The Falling-asleep (Dormition) of the Most Holy Theotokos (August 15/28)

After the Ascension of our Lord, the Holy Theotokos lived with St. John the Beloved in his home. He loved her like his own mother, and she loved him and all of the apostles, and all Christians, like her own children.

One day, as she prayed on the Mount of Olives, an angel told her that in three days she would join our Lord in Paradise, and he gave her a palm branch from Paradise. She returned home to prepare herself, and after a few days, a cloud formed around her home, and angels transported the apostles to her side. She blessed each of them and said goodbye, then lay down on her bed and fell asleep in the Lord.

There was a beautiful funeral procession: first, St. John the Beloved carried the branch from Paradise, and then St. Peter carried the censer. All the Apostles and so many people who loved Mary sang beautiful hymns and brought her to her tomb at Gethsemane.

BRANCH FROM PARADISE

We might head outside and gather some branches or sticks and then decorate them like the branch from Paradise that the angel brought to the Theotokos and which led the procession at her dormition.

If you cannot access branches, or if you prefer, you might twist branches out of scrap paper or pipe cleaners.

Children can then use whatever supplies you have on hand to decorate their branch: they might paint it and cover it with glitter or plastic gemstones; they might draw and cut out leaves or fruits and glue them on.

Resources

Tending the Heart of Virtue: How Classic Stories Awaken a Child's Moral Imagination by Vigen Gourian (Oxford University Press, 1998)

Children in the Church Today: An Orthodox Perspective by Sr. Magdalen (SVS, 1997)

Raising Them Right by St. Theophan the Recluse (Conciliar Press/AFP)

Walking in Wonder: Nurturing Orthodox Christian Virtues in Your Children by Elizabeth White (Conciliar Press/AFP, 2004)

Following A Sacred Path: Raising Godly Children by Elizabeth White (AFP, 2013)

Fasting as a Family: Planning & Preparing Delicious Lenten Meals by Melissa Naasko (AFP, 2016)

The Ascetic Lives of Mothers: A Prayer Book for Orthodox Moms by Annalisa Boyd (AFP, 2014)

The Ancient Faith Prayer Book (AFP, 2014)

A Child's Guide to the Divine Liturgy (AFP, 2014)

Heaven Meets Earth: Celebrating Pascha and the Twelve Feasts by John Skinas (AFP, 2015)

Celebrating the Twelve Days of Christmas: A Family Devotional in the Eastern Orthodox Tradition by AmandaEve Wigglesworth (Conciliar Press/AFP, 2012)

A large selection of icons and supplies for your home altar are available at store.ancientfaith.com."

Notes

1   St. John Chrysostom, *On Marriage and Family Life*, trans. Catharine P. Roth & David Anderson (Crestwood, NY: St. Vladimir's Seminary Press, 1986), p. 67.

2   Mickle, Protodeacon Leonid, "Cultivating That Quiet Light," *Orthodox America*, web. 15 July, 2015.

3   Raffan, Fr. John, trans., *Wounded by Love: The Life and Wisdom of Elder Porphyrios* (Limni, Evia, Greece: Denise Harvey, 2005), p. 196.

4   "America's Changing Religious Landscape," Pew Research Center. May 12, 2005. Web. 20 July, 2015.

5   St. John Chrysostom, op. cit., p. 57.

6   Elder Paisios of Mount Athos, *Spiritual Counsels, vol. IV: Family Life*, trans. Chamberas, Fr. Peter, ed. Famellos, Anna and Eleftheria Kaimakliotis. (Greece: Holy Monastery Evangelist John the Theologian, 2002), p. 164.

7   St. John of Kronstadt, *My Life in Christ*, trans. Goulaeff, E.E. (Jordanville, NY: Holy Trinity Monastery Press, 1984), p. 155.

8   Archimandrite Vasileios of Iveron, *The Thunderbolt of Ever-Living Fire* (Alhambra, CA: Sebastian Press, 2014), p. 20.

9   *The Way of the Pilgrim; and the Pilgrim Continues on His Way*, trans. Savin, Olga (Boston, MA: Shambhala Publications, Inc., 2001), p. 74.

10 St. John Chrysostom, op. cit., p. 72.

11 Allen, Kevin, interview with Hieromonk Damascene, "Fr. Seraphim Rose—The Man, the Struggler." Ancient Faith Ministries. 2007. Web. 4 June, 2015.

12 Rose, Laurence, ed., *Fr. Seraphim Rose Speaks: Excerpts from His*

Writings. Orthodox Christian Information Center. http://orthodox-info.com/praxis/frseraphimspeaks.aspx web, 8/1/2015).

13   Palmer, G.E.H. with P. Sherrard and K. Ware, eds. and trans., *The Philokalia: The Complete Text* (London and Boston: Faber & Faber, 1979), p. 319.

14   Schmemann, Alexander, *For the Life of the World* (Crestwood, NY: SVS Press, 1973), p. 27.

15   Sr. Magdalen, *Children in the Church Today* (Crestwood, NY: SVS Press, 1991), p. 61.

16   Lewis, C. S., *The Screwtape Letters* (New York: Harper Collins Publishers, 1942), p. 6.

17   Elder Paisios the Athonite, op. cit., p. 171.

18   St. John of Kronstadt, op. cit.

19   Elder Paisios the Athonite, op. cit.

20   Tzoganakis, Evangelos, "The Life of Father Seraphim Rose." *Eastern Orthodox Spirituality*, 8, May 2014. Web. 15 July 2015.

21   Mileant, Bishop Alexander, "Ambrose: Elder of Optina," trans. Larin, Seraphim. Fr. Alexander. Web. 15 July 2015.

22   St. Theophan the Recluse, "Theophan the Recluse, On Prayer, Homily 1," trans. van Opstall, Fr. Michael. Monachos.net January 2007. Web. 7 July 2015.

23   Elder Paisios the Athonite, op. cit., pp. 166–167.

24   St. Theophan the Recluse, *Orthodox Life vol. 32, no. 4*. Trans. Pavlenko, Stefan. (July–August 1982). P. 24.

25   St. Seraphim of Sarov, "Spiritual Instructions for Laymen and Monks," *The Little Russian Philokalia, vol. 1: St Seraphim of Sarov* (New Valaam, AK: St. Herman Press, 1991).

26   *The Philokalia*, op. cit., p. 17.

27   Schaff, Philip, ed. *Nicene and Post-Nicene Fathers, First Series, Vol. IX* (New York: Cosimo, 2007), p. 359.

28   A monk of the Eastern Church, *The Year of Grace of the Lord* (Crestwood, NY: SVS Press), pp. 1–3.

29   *Nicene and Post-Nicene Fathers*, op. cit., p. 359.

30   Mileant, Archimandrite Alexander, ed., "On Fasting" Lessons from the Fathers. Missionary Leaflet #Eec. 13 October, 1997. Web. 15 July 2015.

31   Lewis, C. S., op. cit., pp. 60-61.

32   *The Philokalia*, op. cit., p. 320.

33   *The Philokalia*, op. cit., p. 179

34 St. John of Kronstadt, op. cit.

35 Seppala, "The Compassionate Mind: Science shows why it's healthy and how it spreads," in *Observer*, Vol. 26, no. 25, June/July 2013.

36 Lewis, C. S., *Mere Christianity* (New York: HarperCollins Publishers, 1952), p. 86.

37 Sr. Magdalen, op. cit., pp. 88–89.

38 Sr. Magdalen, op. cit., pp. 89–90.

39 *Wounded by Love*, op. cit., p. 198.

40 *Wounded by Love*, op. cit., p. 198.

41 *Wounded by Love*, op. cit., p. 204.

42 St. John Chrysostom, op. cit., p. 71.

43 An excellent resource for understanding and celebrating the Twelve Great Feasts is the fully illustrated book *Heaven Meets Earth*, available from store.ancientfaith.com. For each feast, the book includes an icon with explanation, a summary of the feast's significance, the scripture readings and hymns for the feast, traditions for home celebration, and more.

About the Authors

Elissa Bjeletich hosts the popular Ancient Faith Radio podcast, *Raising Saints: Educating Our Youth in the Orthodox Faith, Both at Home and in the Parish*. She is the author of *In God's Hands: A Mother's Journey through Her Infant's Critical Illness* (Ancient Faith Publishing, 2013) and the Sunday school director at Transfiguration Greek Orthodox Church. She lives near Austin, Texas, with her husband, Marko, and their five daughters.

Caleb Shoemaker is the father of four children. A graduate of Gordon College with a BA in Youth Ministries and an MA in Biblical Languages from Gordon-Conwell Theological Seminary, Caleb has worked in church and parachurch ministry for seventeen years. He and his wife Emily converted to Orthodoxy in 2012. He blogs very sporadically about the importance of bringing the life of the church and the life of the family together at www.calebshoemaker.com. This is his first book.

Ancient Faith Publishing hopes you have enjoyed and benefited from this book. The proceeds from the sales of our books only partially cover the costs of operating our nonprofit ministry—which includes both the work of **Ancient Faith Publishing** and the work of **Ancient Faith Radio.** Your financial support makes it possible to continue this ministry both in print and online. Donations are tax-deductible and can be made at www.ancientfaith. com.

To request a catalog of other publications,
please call us at (800) 967-7377 or (219) 728-2216
or log onto our website: **store.ancientfaith.com**

Bringing you Orthodox Christian music, readings,
prayers, teaching, and podcasts 24 hours a day since 2004 at
www.ancientfaith.com